Moral Philosophy and Moral Education

Moral Philosophy and Moral Education

Thora Ilin Bayer

CASCADE *Books* • Eugene, Oregon

MORAL PHILOSOPHY AND MORAL EDUCATION

Copyright © 2017 Thora Ilin Bayer. All rights reserved. Except for brief quotations in critical publications or reviews, no part of this book may be reproduced in any manner without prior written permission from the publisher. Write: Permissions, Wipf and Stock Publishers, 199 W. 8th Ave., Suite 3, Eugene, OR 97401.

Cascade Books
An Imprint of Wipf and Stock Publishers
199 W. 8th Ave., Suite 3
Eugene, OR 97401

www.wipfandstock.com

PAPERBACK ISBN: 978-1-5326-0459-1
HARDCOVER ISBN: 978-1-5326-0461-4
EBOOK ISBN: 978-1-5326-0460-7

Cataloguing-in-Publication data:

Names: Bayer, Thora Ilin, 1966–.

Title: Moral philosophy and moral education / Thora Ilin Bayer.

Description: Eugene, OR: Cascade Books, 2017 | Includes bibliographical references and index.

Identifiers: ISBN 978-1-5326-0459-1 (paperback) | ISBN 978-1-5326-0461-4 (hardcover) | ISBN 978-1-5326-0460-7 (ebook)

Subjects: LCSH: Education—Philosophy | Moral education

Classification: LC191 B192 2017 (print) | LC191 (ebook)

Manufactured in the U.S.A. 05/15/17

In the night of thick darkness enveloping
the earliest antiquity, so remote from ourselves,
there shines the eternal and never failing
light of a truth beyond all question: that
the world of civil society has certainly been
made by human beings, and that its principles
are therefore to be found within the modifications
of our own human mind.

—Giambattista Vico

Contents

Preface | ix
Introduction: Philosophical Idealism | xi

1 Moral Philosophy and Culture | 1
2 Culture and History | 19
3 Human Nature and Education | 36
4 Pragmatism and Idealism | 50
5 The Phenomenology of Spirit as *Bildungsroman* | 66
6 Rhetoric and Human Education | 85
7 The Aesthetic Dimension of Education | 109
8 Education for the Common Good | 124

Bibliography | 131
Index | 135

Preface

This work considers the interconnections of education, ethics, and culture as aspects of the distinctively human concern with self-knowledge. Its sources for the comprehension of these topics are in the tradition of philosophical idealism, conceived as having its beginnings in Plato, extending through Italian humanism to Hegel and to Cassirer's philosophy of symbolic forms. So often, moral philosophy is approached *sui generis* without regard for its relation to the nature of human education and the philosophy of culture. The individual human self finds its inner life writ large in the forms of culture, such as religion, art, and history. The individual looks toward such forms of cultural life as representing the normative ideals that can shape character and the conduct of civic life.

At the basis of civic life and individual character is the education of the human spirit. The Greeks understood such education as *paideia*, the view that education aims at the production in the individual of a broad mental outlook harmoniously joined with cultural development. The Italian humanists put this forth in the ideal of intellectual eloquence expressed in the phrase, *la sapienza che parla* (wisdom speaking). The German idealist philosophers sought to preserve this sense of education through the concept of *Bildung*. This distinctively German term connotes the education of the whole person and is distinct from education conceived as a process of training in a particular skill, subject matter, or occupation. The education of the human spirit appears in the literary tradition as the idea of *Bildungsroman*—a work dedicated to presenting the reader with the self-formation of the individual. It is a term that can be applied to the philosophical views considered in this work.

Education in the sense of *paideia* and *Bildung* gives us access to culture, and culture gives us access to those norms and ideals that have developed in the history of humanity. It is within the means of philosophy to examine

Preface

these and to put them before us for our consideration. The purpose of this work is to bring forth the connections between human education and human culture as the context of moral philosophy and, in so doing, to place the issues involved in both historical and systematic perspective.

My aim is not to close off this subject in the manner of a moral treatise but in the chapters that follow to go over a common ground in various ways. My wish is to prompt the reader to consider the issues in the reader's own terms. There is no proper finality in the philosophical and moral enterprise. The approach of Socrates, of seeking to ask the right questions and pursuing their answers by remaining open to all the possibilities they entail, still stands at the center of all true philosophy.

The philosophical examples of *Bildungsroman* upon which I principally draw are those of the Christian humanism of the Italian tradition, in particular the *New Science* of Giambattista Vico, and the German tradition of philosophical idealism, in particular Hegel's conception of a phenomenology of spirit and Cassirer's philosophy of symbolic forms as grounded in his metaphysics of a dialectic of spirit and life. I regard the thought of Vico, Hegel, and Cassirer as a continuum that may be conceived as philosophical idealism in its broadest sense. Associated with this continuum are the views of education to be found in classic American pragmatism, especially in the philosophy of John Dewey. These great traditions have at their core a vision of moral education centered in a philosophy of culture. The chapters of this work take the reader through the various aspects of the philosophy of culture, leading to the final view of education for the common good, placing the individual within the human community.

I thank the Institute for Vico Studies at Emory University for the use of its library and facilities made available to me through summer fellowships while writing this work. I also express my gratitude to the RosaMary Foundation at Xavier University of Louisiana for generous funding that has continually supported my research.

Introduction

Philosophical Idealism

As indicated in the Preface, I conceive moral philosophy and moral education within the context of philosophical idealism and the approach to human culture that lies within it. My aim in the following remarks is to articulate a view of the inner form of this type of philosophical thinking. It is the standpoint from which the views of the succeeding chapters arise. These chapters pass back and forth between historical sources and systematic issues in an attempt to keep each of these in touch with the other. The reader will find that these chapters at times go over the same ground more than once but do so from different perspectives. This style is an attempt always to keep the central issues in mind. Philosophy depends on memory and on seeing that the True is an interconnected whole.

Philosophical idealism as it developed in the works of Kant and Hegel in the latter part of the eighteenth and first decades of the nineteenth century involved an interest in culture as connected to forms of human knowledge. Kant employed the word *Cultur* and wrote an *Anthropology* as well as making an important contribution to speculative philosophy of history in his essay, "Idea of a Universal History from a Cosmopolitan View."[1] Hegel employed the term *Geist* in place of culture as the overarching term for his "science of the experience of consciousness" of the *Phenomenology of Spirit* and along with Vico before him, in his masterpiece the *New Science of the Common Nature of the Nations*, founded the field of the philosophy of history. Kant held a view of human education that is implicit in his moral philosophy and views of history and is directly expressed in his "Lecture Notes on Pedagogy" as did Hegel in his developmental view of human con-

---

1. Kant employs *Cultur* instead of *Kultur*. For development of the idea of culture, especially in German philosophy, see Kroeber and Kluckhohn, *Culture*.

sciousness and in his lecture "On Classical Studies" delivered while Rector of the Gymnasium at Nüremberg.

To this tradition we may add in the twentieth century Cassirer's *Philosophy of Symbolic Forms* and his later summary and restating of it in *An Essay on Man*. Cassirer's philosophical idealism is derived both from Kant and Hegel, joining Kant's transcendental approach to the object with Hegel's developmental approach to the internal dialectic of the subject. In his 1936 lecture to the Warburg Institute in London, "Critical Idealism as a Philosophy of Culture," Cassirer connects the philosophy of culture not only to Kant but also to Hegel's *Phenomenology* and sees both of these senses of idealism as originating in the Platonic philosophy of form or *eidos*, *idea*. Cassirer transforms idealism, the philosophy of the idea, into the philosophy of the symbol. He holds that the "clue" to the nature of the human is the symbol and redefines the human from *animal rationale* to *animal symbolicum*. Human culture comes about through the distinctively human art of reacting to and affecting the environment or *Umwelt* in terms of the system of symbols that constitutes culture. The primary principle of human education implicit in Cassirer's work is the pursuit of self-knowledge not as a project of psychological introspection but as a process of *Bildung* in which the particular individual confronts the self writ large in the symbolic forms of culture—myth and religion, language, art, history, science, and social forms such as politics, economics, and ethics.

In addition to the works of Kant and Hegel, one of the great sources for Cassirer is Vico's *New Science*. Cassirer relied on Vico as well as Schelling in his theory of myth as the primordial symbolic form from which culture develops. Cassirer calls Vico the "real discoverer of the myth."[2] Cassirer's reference is to Vico's doctrine of *la sapienza poetica*, "poetic wisdom." In it Vico shows that Plato's original separation of the form or *eidos* from the image or *eikōn* that results in the so-called ancient quarrel between philosophy and poetry can be resolved by conceiving philosophy as developing from poetry, rather than regarding poetry as a defective form of philosophy. Vico's poetic wisdom or what in contemporary terms would be called "mythical thought," the term Cassirer uses, is presupposed by the discursive thought of the idea. Culture, like the world of the child, first forms objects through the activity of the imagination or *fantasia*. As Vico shows, *universali fantastici* "imaginative universals" precede *universali intelligibili* "intelligible or abstract universals." Any "nation" or culture in its beginnings forms the

---

2. Cassirer, *Problem of Knowledge*, 296.

INTRODUCTION

world in terms of certain master images that later become thoughts, just as the world of childhood images give way to conceptual language.

Like Kant, Hegel, and Cassirer, Vico before them has in his philosophy of culture a doctrine of human education that includes moral education. In his oration on *The Study Methods of Our Time* (1708/09), Vico says that children's minds must first be exposed to the forms of the imagination and memory and only later in their development should they proceed to abstract forms of reasoning. Euclidean or plane geometry is suitable for young children because of its use of figures but analytic geometry should not be introduced at an early age as it requires a mind capable of pure abstractions.[3]

Vico, like Cassirer, sees self-knowledge as the aim of education in the sense, as he declares in his first university oration on education in 1699, of the student passing through the whole cycle of the fields of human knowledge.[4] Vico says that "the whole is really the flower of wisdom."[5] This sense of the importance of the whole has a resonance with Hegel's dictum that *Das Wahre ist das Ganze*—the True is the whole. Hegel's *Phenomenology* in which consciousness develops itself through all these stages of spirit is, as mentioned above, a philosophical *Bildungsroman* in which the human self realizes itself by confronting all of its possible stances on the object before it. The self achieves an inner life by confronting all that is there outside it and realizes that what is actually there is itself, its own nature writ large.

A further principal figure to be considered, as mentioned in the Preface, is Dewey, whose views of culture, education, and ethics are like that of Cassirer. Dewey was influenced by Hegel and was a contemporary of Cassirer. The connection between Cassirer and Dewey is the subject of Chapter 3. Although Cassirer does not share Dewey's pragmatic transformation of German idealism, he does share something of the sense of pluralism in pragmatism. In *An Essay on Man*, Cassirer quotes in two places, with essential agreement, from Dewey's *Human Nature and Conduct* and *Experience and Nature*. In considering questions with which this work is concerned, Dewey is a figure that cannot be overlooked.

Moral education is crucial for philosophy. In Plato's myth of the cave, the Socratic figure on returning to the cave begins to teach its occupants what is outside the cave, an activity that Plato properly designates as

---

3. Vico, *Study Methods*, 6–9.
4. Vico, *Humanistic Education*, 33–52.
5. Vico, *Study Methods*, 77.

dangerous. The truth of the whole is realized by those who have a vision of it through their attempt to communicate it to others. Philosophy is a process of rational intercourse and it requires the human practice of friendship. In Plato's case it results in the "friends of the forms." In the original oath of Hippocrates, one of the duties stated by the physician is to pass the knowledge of the body on to the children of other physicians. The doctor of the body is to pass on the knowledge of the body and its healing to others. The philosopher or "lover of wisdom" (*philosophos*) is the doctor of the soul (*psychē*) and the philosopher has a similar duty. For its continuance philosophy requires its conveyance to others. In so doing, it provides views of human education and the importance of virtue as the basis of human conduct. The ancient precepts of the temple of Apollo at Delphi *gnothi seauton* "know thyself" and the moral admonition *mēden agan* "nothing overmuch" live on in true philosophy and can enter into the general approach to education that is implicit in philosophical exchange, whether it be in the ancient Socratic form of *elenchos* or in the modern form of discourse.

The problem inherent in most modern theories of education is that they are formulated as a set of procedures unconnected to any overall philosophy of culture. There are no explicit ideals that guide this theory. Education moves from one theory to another in a kind of Platonic world of appearance without a grounding in human culture itself that can establish what A. N. Whitehead called in the title of his classic, *The Aims of Education*. The aims of education for Whitehead are derived from his conceptions in *Adventures of Ideas* and *Religion in the Making* that advocate a view of civilization and the ideas that guide it. Without this sense of ideas and the ideals to which they point, no true theory of education can be formulated. In saying this I do not mean that there is only one theory of education that is tenable. I am only suggesting the conditions required for a viable theory of education. My pluralism holds here as in the philosophy of culture and symbolic forms. A theory of education requires the results of the social and behavioral sciences as well as the experience gained in the practice of educating. But in addition these approaches need to be joined with the philosophical examination of human ideals that ground education within human culture.

In another small book, *The Function of Reason*, Whitehead distinguishes between two senses of reason—that of Odysseus and that of Plato.[6]

---

6. Whitehead, *Function of Reason*, 10.

Introduction

The wily Odysseus, the man of all guises, makes his way home to Ithaca from Troy by finding a solution to every problematic situation he encounters. His reason is practical, problem-solving reason. Plato's reason is speculative, a power that allows him to think with the gods, to pass beyond the seen and to grasp the unseen—what is permanent beyond the changeable and impermanent. Odysseus is a clever man of the world, a hero of action. Plato, to use Vico's term, is a heroic mind. He appears to us as a spirit who has come to stay for a while in the world. He is Kant's "light dove."[7] Whitehead's distinction is parallel to the distinction Isaiah Berlin makes in the history of ideas between the hedgehog and the fox.[8] The hedgehog knows one big thing. The fox knows many things. Platonic reason knows one thing—the Good that dominates the world of *eidē*. Odysseus knows many things and can always adapt what he knows to the practical problem at hand. He is wily and cunning. He has a version of what Hegel calls the "cunning of reason," the power of reason to wind its way through the details of experience.

Philosophical idealism, as Cassirer claims, has its ancient origin in the Platonic doctrine of the idea. Philosophical idealism is a hedgehog. It perceives reason as a means to grasp the whole of things, to attain the absolute mode of thought. It differs in its aim and its object from those movements that have dominated twentieth-century philosophy—linguistic analysis, descriptive phenomenology, secular hermeneutics, structuralism, and deconstruction. These movements share with Odysseus a focus on that part of experience that can be the subject of their particular kind of ingenuity and method. They are not driven by an aim to attain the great principles of moral philosophy and moral education—the True, Good, and Beautiful. They work within their problematic sense of experience. They have, however, one great difference with Odysseus. They have no Ithaca. Odysseus's actions are all directed to his need to arrive home, to transcend the conditions of his journey in the way that the self of the journey of Hegel's phenomenology arrives at its terminus of absolute knowing that arises from the stage of religion and settles into its true home, the timeless world of the categories of the science of logic.

The abovementioned movements of twentieth-century philosophy are fascinating in their ingenuity but they pale before the Socratic question of their purpose. Hermeneutics, for example, as a means for bringing forth the meaning of biblical scripture presupposes the sacredness of the text.

---

7. Kant, *Critique of Pure Reason*, 47.
8. Berlin, *Hedgehog and the Fox*, 1–4.

Introduction

Secular hermeneutics can also bring forth the meaning of texts or institutions treated as texts, but has no answer to the question of what texts or institutions are worth hermeneutical investigation. The value of hermeneutics cannot be answered hermeneutically. To the Socratic question of the ultimate value of hermeneutics, hermeneutics simply stands mute. The same can be said of deconstruction. Once the great narratives have been deconstructed we are free of their illusions and stand before the world, the scales fallen from our eyes. Then what? If what was deconstructed was not the True, what was or is the True? And, how is it connected to the Good and the Beautiful?

As Hegel has pointed out, true freedom is not freedom from constraint; freedom is the power of self-determination of activity toward an ultimate. When we stand back and look carefully at these movements they appear to be the "business" that Hegel describes in his phenomenological stage of "Das geistige Tierreich und der Betrug oder die Sache-selbst"—"the spiritual menagerie and humbug or the matter-in-hand." The spiritual menagerie in Hegel's conception is the world of academic investigators, each involved in a specific project. As long as they are engaged in their projects, thought seems authentic and vital. The Socratic procedure of asking the obvious is put off. But they are haunted by the Socratic question of purpose. Once it is asked, the incessant activity appears to have a hollowness, a void, a lack of wonder (*thauma*). We are at this moment taken back to the presence of the idea, the Plantonic *eidos*, the Vichian *universale fantastico*, the Hegelian *Begriff*, the Cassirerian *symbolische Form*. This return offers us a new beginning point, a way to renew philosophizing in a positive way, to think within and through experience to a sense of what is ultimate and beyond experience, a *Jenseits*, to approach the reality of the divine. Wonder, the original motivation to philosophize, can return as can the possibility of epiphany in our pursuit of a rational grasp of the whole and of the True, Good, and Beautiful.

In the chapters that follow, I have attempted to capture something of the spirit of philosophy that exists in the specific historical, ethical, and epistemological issues I discuss. They are philosophical inquiries done in a traditional manner. I have based my discussions in metaphysical, ethical, and epistemological sources in accord with Cassirer's principle that he states in his preface to the third volume of the *Philosophy of Symbolic Forms*: "the custom, which has once more become popular, of hurling one's ideas into empty space as it were, without inquiring into their relation to the general development of scientific philosophy, has never stuck me as fruitful."⁹ Philosophy requires context and the most complete context for philosophy is its own history.

---

9. Cassirer, *Philosophy of Symbolic Forms*, 3:xvi.

1

Moral Philosophy and Culture

The Philosophy of Culture and the Philosophy of Symbolic Forms

Philosophical idealism since Hegel has had the problem of whether it can produce an ethics or moral philosophy. The philosophy of the idea always risks the propensity to allow thought to withdraw into its own inner form, to develop an account of experience solely in terms of dialectical distinctions and categories. The result can be a metaphysical logic that offers a single system of the real in which the object is brought together with the subject. When this approach is extended to ethics, the result can be a comprehensive system of the existing forms of moral, social, and political life, but no vision of the Good appears forthcoming from philosophy itself. The owl of Minerva, as Hegel says, flies only at the falling of the dusk. Philosophy, then, seems to play no role in the making of the day. How can philosophical idealism overcome these problems? As the argument of this work develops through the following chapters, I wish to suggest that the answer lies in a conception of human education.

Cassirer inherits this problem of philosophical idealism, of the idea bending back upon itself as its own circle, attached to the world only in principle and without any influence on human practice. His first solution is to return to the critical idealism of Kant, but to go further than the Marburg Neo-Kantian preoccupation with science and cognition. Cassirer perceived Kant as laying the groundwork for a philosophy of human culture once it is understood that the task of critical philosophy is to uncover the forms of human experience. The problem of knowledge is the problem of the forms of knowledge. In the first *Critique*, Kant shows the form of theoretical thought, in the second *Critique*, ethical life, and in the third *Critique*, the organic and the aesthetic. Cassirer extends Kantian criticism to myth, religion, language, art, and contemporary science. He also mentions forms of custom (*Sitte*), law (*Recht*), economics (*Wirtschaft*), and technology (*Technik*). Thus, Cassirer says, the critique of reason becomes the critique of culture.

The factor that ties all of these kinds of form together is the symbol. The symbol occurs when something in sense perception takes on universal meaning. Cassirer finds in the phenomenon of the symbol an actualization of "sense" in the "sensible" (*Sinn im Sinnlichkeit*) that is at the basis of the Kantian conception of the "schematism." All forms of knowledge are embodied in basic forms of cultural life, and these are made possible by the power of the symbolic act to grasp meaning in the sensible. Seen this way, Cassirer's philosophy of symbolic forms is a new philosophy of idealism that differs from Hegel's idealism in three fundamental ways.

First, Cassirer says that Hegel's phenomenology of spirit begins too high in experience, at the level of the thing. He purports with his analysis of myth to take Hegel's ladder one step lower, to the level of the expressive function of consciousness, in which the world is first felt as an interaction of malignant and benign forces. Second, through his doctrine of the symbol, Cassirer can resist the tendency to move from the phenomena of spirit (*Geist*) to the idea, in which philosophy becomes a pure process of thought, as he claims occurs in Hegel's *Science of Logic*, in which the individual forms of experience become absorbed in one form, that of metaphysical logic. Third, Cassirer does away with Hegel's principle of the Absolute. He sees the Absolute as forcing all the forms of experience into a single system, in which one form is *aufhoben* into the next, often overriding the confrontations and oppositional gaps that lie within actual cultural development. Cassirer wishes to replace Hegel's dialectic of *Aufhebung* with his dialectic of function, in which, at any point in cultural life, philosophy can give a systematic account of the interrelations of the various symbolic forms without reducing them to an overall logic. Cassirer replaces the idea of system with the idea of systematic review (*systematischer Überblick*).

Cassirer takes from Hegel the view that the forms of spirit are a totality and that the relations between them are dialectical. Cassirer says he agrees with Hegel that "the True is the whole." His conception of "review" or *Überblick* is that these relations are best articulated by passing back and forth among the forms of culture and showing how each specifically functions in relation to the others. Cassirer endorses Hegel's developmental conception of phenomenology over and against purely descriptive phenomenology.

He wishes to show how all human knowledge, as well as each of its forms, develops from a basis in mythical expression to a stage of representational thought and finally to a stage of purely significative thought, in which symbols generate meanings through other systems of symbols.

In order for the critique of reason to become the critique of culture, Cassirer follows in his own thought the course that philosophical idealism took in the history of modern philosophy from Kant to Hegel. In so doing, Cassirer develops an idealism that is neither truly Kantian nor Hegelian. In his intellectual odyssey he sails between the Scylla of Kant and the Charybdis of Hegel. To maintain his course he obtains help from many figures, such as Vico, Herder, Wilhelm von Humboldt, Heinrich Hertz, Theodor Vischer, and from Goethe, to whose thought he turns for many crucial starting points, including his concept of "basis phenomena" (*Basisphänomene*).

Cassirer sees that the Hegelian synthesis depends upon the philosophy of spirit. The central concept of Hegel is *Geist*, which leads to the system, the "idea" of the *Science of Logic*. The reaction to this concept is philosophy of life, *Lebensphilosophie*. Cassirer expands the conception of the philosophy of life beyond the particular movement by that name in German philosophy. Cassirer's expanded concept of the philosophy of life includes the works of Klages, Simmel, Scheler, Bergson, and Heidegger. Life philosophy attempts to solve the problems of the tendency to the idea in the philosophy of spirit by calling attention to the reality of the immediacy of life. Unity lies not in the forms of spirit but in the immediate existence of life.

Cassirer divides the whole of the late nineteenth and twentieth-century philosophy into philosophies of spirit and philosophies of life. It is this metaphysical opposition between spirit and life that Cassirer thinks the philosophy of symbolic forms can overcome. For this solution Cassirer turns to Hegel. He sees Hegel as understanding that spirit is a transformation of life. Life takes on the life of form. Life in its immediacy continues to challenge spirit, and spirit must formulate a continual response to it. The solution Cassirer ultimately advances to the interconnection of life and spirit is his conception of basis phenomena.

Cassirer is brought to the problem of spirit and life not out of purely theoretical concerns but out of essentially moral concerns. Cassirer comes to these problems because of the times. He understood from the beginning that there is a normative dimension to human culture, that the problem of form is connected to the ideal of freedom. His response to World War I was his book, *Freiheit und Form* (Freedom and form), which is an interpretation of German aesthetics and cultural history. Form releases the human spirit from the bonds it is held in through the immediacy of sense. This freedom takes place through the power of art to form our senses and sensibilities. The theme of the power of the symbol to pass beyond the immediate into the mediation of cultural activity runs through Cassirer's treatment of myth, language, and science in the *Philosophy of Symbolic Forms*. But this freedom from the immediate is treated in this work in epistemic terms, not in terms of ethical or cultural ideals. This normative dimension overtly becomes an issue for Cassirer following his departure from Nazi Germany in 1933 and the ensuing World War II.

Cassirer announces this concern with normative philosophy in his address on assuming his professorship at the University of Göteborg in 1935, in which he discusses the sense in which the nature of philosophy itself is a philosophical problem.[1] From this point on, the philosophy of symbolic forms becomes something normative for Cassirer. It becomes something more than resolving the problems of philosophical idealism as left in the tension between Kant and Hegel. How does Cassirer accomplish this new turn in his philosophy?

I wish to suggest that he makes this turn by employing Goethe's conception of immediacy and the human to recover a version of Socratic philosophy. In the last decade of his life Cassirer comes to see his philosophy of symbolic forms as a form of Socratic thought that lets him surmount the problems of the distance philosophical idealism has from the world and from human action in the world. The crucial turning points in this process are his views in his 1935 lecture, his conception of the metaphysics of symbolic forms (c. 1940) and his *An Essay on Man* (1944). In his chapter on Hegel in his last work, *The Myth of the State* (1946), which appeared after his death, what concerns Cassirer greatly is the sense in which Hegel's dictum that philosophies are their own times apprehended in thoughts contains a conception of philosophy that promotes only a passive role in relation of the world. It is a role, Cassirer points out, that is not followed by Hegel in his specific political writings, which directly concern constitutional criticism and reforms.

---

1. Cassirer, *Symbol, Myth, and Culture*, 49–63.

Philosophy's Moral Relation to the World

Cassirer's essay "The Concept of Philosophy as a Philosophical Problem" is based on a quotation from Goethe's *Materialien zur Geschichte der Farbenlehre* (*Materials on the History of the Doctrine of Colors*) concerning the difference between Plato and Aristotle. From this he moves to Kant's distinction between a scholastic and a worldly concept of philosophy, and finally he connects this to Schweitzer's concept of the duty philosophy has to society.

Plato, Goethe says, "relates himself to the world as a blessed spirit, whom it pleases sometimes to stay for awhile in the world; he is not so much concerned to come to know the world, because he already presupposes it, as to communicate to it in a friendly way what he brings along with him and what it needs."[2] Plato investigates the world in order to see beyond it, to rise in his thinking to its heights in order to return to its origin. Aristotle, Goethe says, on the contrary: "stands to the world as a man, an architect. He is only here once and must here make and create. He inquires about the earth, but not farther than to find a ground. . . . He draws a huge circumference for his building, procures materials from all sides, arranges them, piles them up, and climbs thus in regular form, pyramid fashion to the top."[3] Aristotle is of the world, inquiring into it on its own terms, reconstructing it as a hierarchical ordering of its forms. Cassirer says that these two opposed tendencies run throughout the development of philosophical thought. "Both of the souls," Cassirer says, "abide in almost all great thinkers."[4] They are the two sides of Faust—one that clings to what is here in the world and the other that struggles to transcend the world with a sublime vision.

Cassirer claims a significant moment in the history of philosophy, in which these two opposed powers are placed in balance, is the Kantian critical philosophy. Kant takes up the Platonic tendency toward form and redirects it, from its flight to a supersensible world, to an elucidation of the principles of the empirical world of experience, which are themselves not empirical but *a priori*. Like Aristotle, Cassirer says, Kant "stands firmly on the well-grounded earth, on the certain ground of science, but at the same time he wishes to lay bare the last supporting layer on which this

---

2. Ibid., 50–51.
3. Ibid., 51.
4. Ibid., 51–52.

foundation of the edifice of science rests."[5] Cassirer says that the position of critical philosophy is decisive for him, but from this standpoint philosophy must raise the problem of the whole. He says, "Philosophy cannot be satisfied to ask about the form and structure of particular cultural regions, about the structure of language, art, law, myth, and religion. The deeper it penetrates into this structure the more clear and the more urgent becomes the problem of the whole for it. [Philosophy must ask:] What is this whole of spiritual culture? What is its end, its goal, its meaning?"[6]

Cassirer says whenever this question of the whole is asked, philosophy can face it only through self-reflection. The question of the whole, which is essentially a Hegelian question, leads directly to the normative role of philosophy. To determine the meaning of culture is to advance a view of its goal and to suggest action in relation to its goal. In this way philosophy becomes involved in the world as a result of pursuing its own form of inquiry that is a comprehension of the whole of culture, the whole of the activity of the human spirit.

Cassirer calls attention to the twofold conception of philosophy stated in "The Architectonic of Pure Reason" in the first *Critique*. Kant speaks of the "scholastic conception" of philosophy. This is the pursuit of philosophy of its own ends—the logical perfection of knowledge, the lawful arrangement of principles, of proofs, and of the systematic unity of knowledge. This scholastic conception of philosophy cannot be dispensed with. This conception is essential for the dedication to reason that characterizes the philosopher. In addition to this scholastic conception of philosophy there is, Kant says, another conception of philosophy, a *conceptus cosmicus*. Kant says, "On this view, philosophy is the science of the relation of all knowledge to the essential ends of human reason (*teleologia rationis humanae*), and the philosopher is not an artificer in the field of reason, but himself the lawgiver of human reason."[7] Cassirer says we have left this ideal behind in the development of modern philosophy, and he asks whether it is an ideal simply tied to the eighteenth-century doctrine of enlightenment or whether it is a part of philosophy itself when it conceives of the ideal of the philosopher.

---

5. Ibid., 53.
6. Ibid., 57.
7. Ibid., 58–59.

Cassirer turns for an answer to Albert Schweitzer, whom he calls "one of the true cultural philosophers of our time."[8] Schweitzer's view is expressed in his lectures delivered at the University of Uppsala in 1922, between the two world wars. Schweitzer reproaches contemporary philosophy for not seeing the crumbling of the ethical ideals of culture and warning us. Cassirer says he does not absolve himself from an attachment to the scholastic concept of philosophy. Indeed, this lecture is a definite turning point in Cassirer's concern with the normative possibilities of the philosophy of symbolic forms, a turn from it being simply a theory of knowledge to being a philosophical ideal. Schweitzer says that philosophy is not to be blamed for the crisis of modern culture. Philosophy did not cause the disintegration of ethical ideals, but it failed in its duty to warn us. He says, "in the hour of peril the watchman slept, who should have kept watch over us. So it happened that we did not struggle for our culture."[9]

At the end of his inaugural lecture Cassirer criticizes Hegel for the unjustified optimism of the dictum "What is rational is real; what is real is rational." He says reason is never a mere present, something simply actual. Reason must be actualized. It is not a given but a task. Cassirer says this view of reason as task holds in not only the theoretical sphere but also in the practical sphere. Culture is made by us as a struggle for the form of our own humanity. Here in this view Cassirer foreshadows his view of culture as self-knowledge and as tied to the basis phenomenon of the work (*das Werk*) in his metaphysics.

In his essay, "Critical Idealism as a Philosophy of Culture," Cassirer carries this point further. He says that the universal theme of the philosophy of culture and of idealism as connected to it is freedom. Cassirer says, "This aim is a moral one: and it is, therefore, in morality, it is in the system of ethics that we have to seek the true principles of a philosophy of history and a philosophy of civilization."[10] Freedom, Cassirer says, is tied to the autonomy of reason and this is the universal aim of a philosophy of culture. He says that Hegel and Kant agree on the importance of reason's relation to human freedom.

Hegel's philosophy involves an attack on Kant's idealism but, Cassirer says, there is one point on which Kant and Hegel perfectly agree. He says: "Like Kant he is convinced that the problem of freedom is the beginning

8. Ibid., 59.
9. Ibid., 60.
10. Ibid., 85.

and end of idealistic philosophy. This problem pervades the whole work of Hegel."[11] Cassirer says that the unity of culture is both an idea and an ideal, both of which must be understood dynamically. Both Hegel and Kant hold that the "process of culture is the progress of the consciousness of freedom."[12] The attempt to make this principle of freedom known, to recover it from the basis of idealism, is Cassirer's version of the philosophical watchman. But he is always conscious that the power of the call to awake is tied to the ability of philosophy to maintain its "scholastic" stance. Ethical ideals that are not underpinned by a valid concept of knowledge and human reality will lose their ability to convince.

Basis Phenomena

To accomplish the view that reason is the self-renewing work of spirit and that the essence of history is freedom, Cassirer needs a philosophy of life that will allow him to preserve the immediacy of life yet allow spirit (*Geist*) to arise naturally from life (*Leben*). A doctrine of freedom must be attached not simply to the flow of life but to the forms of culture as they arise in spirit. The idea or form must be grounded in what is not the idea as such. It must be grounded in what is primary in human experience.

To discover what is primary, Cassirer turns to Goethe. In his Maxims 391–93, Goethe declares three phenomena to be basic to human existence. The first is life, which he describes as "the rotating movement of the monad itself." He says that the impulse to nurture this life is implanted in every individual but what it is in itself is a mystery. The second phenomenon is "the living-moving monad's intervention into the surroundings of the outer world." The individual being is aware of itself as having no internal limits but as encountering external limits. We can be clear to ourselves about what we experience in the movement of life, but this internality is a mystery to others. We are for them, and they are for us, externals. The third phenomenon is "what we direct toward the outer world as actions and deed, as speech and writing."[13] These are the productions made from our inner world that acquire an independent status beyond ourselves. The outer world can come to have an understanding of these productions that is beyond what we ourselves are able to have. Since an action or thought pro-

---

11. Ibid., 88.
12. Ibid., 90.
13. Cassirer, *Philosophy of Symbolic Forms*, 4:127.

duced from inner reality endures, others may find in it more significance than its creator intended or was aware.

Human life is always, in some sense, conscious of itself; it always "knows itself." Goethe understands these three phenomena as three levels of development. Life as the reality of the monadic being is constant movement. It is the "stream of consciousness" that knows no rest. It is not a "mysterium" in the sense of something completely unknown because it is always revealing itself. It is primary because there is no "explanation" of it as such.

The second level is "becoming aware," which is at the basis of doing, of acting and reacting to surroundings. Life does not remain enclosed within its own circle. It comes forth to the outside and manifests and verifies its existence. This movement of life from the monad to what is external is the basis of the social world and ethical life. There is no reason for this, no causal explanation, because any such understanding is based on the fact of this as a basic phenomenon of the movement of life of the individual. The individual is an abstraction. There is no individual apart from the world it is in. We only recognize ourselves in others.

The third level answers the question of how others know us. They know us only by means of what we do and say, through what we create. "Others can know us only in our work, as what we do and make, as what we say and write, as *praxis* and *poiesis*."[14] "Work" here is the German *Werk*, something made, a product that carries cultural, intellectual, or artistic meaning, not *Arbeit*, the ordinary labor of human existence. The transformation of our internal life into an enduring work that exists for others in an external order is alienating. The "I" of the inward life can no longer find itself and is inclined to move back into itself. These three levels form a circle of human experience upon which human culture is based. They are the metaphysical ground, phenomenologically derived, upon which Cassirer's philosophy of symbolic forms is based.

Goethe, Cassirer says, as an artist protests against any attempt to go behind these primary phenomena. As an artist he is concerned with the surface of the phenomena, and even as a thinker he refuses any attempt at their explanation. Cassirer says Goethe "rages against the 'Procuress Understanding'" that would disrupt the immediacy of life. "The understanding is always at work to mediate this immediacy, but thereby depriving it of its true and original meaning by this alleged mediation."[15] Cassirer claims

---

14. Ibid., 130.
15. Ibid., 132.

that Goethe, as an artist, can hold to this attitude toward the understanding. Cassirer holds that these basis phenomena can have no further philosophical justification, but that it is not possible to eliminate the powers of the understanding as part of our general intellectual life.

On Cassirer's view there is a dialectical relationship between life and spirit as opposite dimensions of the real. Life completes its activity by transforming itself into spirit. Spirit takes up the movement of life into its own activity of the formation of experience. Cassirer emphasizes that life and spirit are not two substances but are functions that interact with each other and mutually determine each other. Life is constantly involved with the mediation of spirit, and spirit is constantly renewing its activity of cultural formation by confrontation with the immediacy of life. Cassirer regards this general metaphysical process as occurring in parallel fashion within the basis phenomena of human existence. The stream of consciousness of life within the "I" mediates itself through action and the will in confrontation with the Other. Beyond the oppositions of social life is the moment of self-reflection from which the work is generated.

In this way Cassirer places the understanding as the manifestation of self-reflection within the dialectic of life and spirit. Self-reflection is rooted, for Cassirer, in the understanding's function of questioning, which is one of the original and vital functions of the mind. The mind truly becomes itself through its power to formulate the question. Cassirer says: "This function stands at the beginning of all philosophy (not only at the beginning of so-called metaphysics)—wonder as the beginning of philosophy. It begins with the question of 'what is.'"[16] Once the question has been formed it is the onset of reflection, which Cassirer sees as the genius of Socrates. Socrates, he says, directs the question from "what is" toward moral self-consciousness: he asks about the "what for," about the *eidos* as *telos*. "The transfiguration of 'life' through the form of the 'question': that is the specifically Socratic achievement."[17]

The device of the question allows Cassirer to formulate an original basis for Kant's conception of reason as related to human aims—reason as lawgiver. Cassirer sees Socrates as providing, in the ethical question, the device that takes us out of theory. The question bridges the gap between the "what is" and the "what for." The question becomes the key to understanding self-reflection as the essential act of human freedom.

16. Ibid., 133.
17. Ibid.

The question takes us out of both the stream of consciousness of life of the "I" and the actions in our response to the Other because the reflective question is an act of self-determination. It removes us from the immediate by objectifying the immediate and thus creating distance between the I and the immediate. The immediate is not just acted on. It can be held at a distance by the mind.

This sense of freedom is both Kantian and Hegelian, but Cassirer finds its roots in Socratic philosophy, which is the original form of the philosophy of the idea. Life and thought stand in a dialectical relationship to each other and thought stands in a dialectical relationship to itself, to its own productions. The question that arises in the philosophical passion of wonder has a counterpart in the answer that is sought and toward which the question directs its attention. But any answer, in Socratic fashion, is only a new standpoint of thought to which the question may be applied. The movement that is inherent in the stream of consciousness is transformed into the movement thought produces within itself, the movement of the idea. In this movement thought attempts to produce its own nature as an object for itself. But the source of its own movement is not simply itself as thought: the constant movement of life within the I is always outstripping the form given it by thought. This movement of life within the I is what moves thought forward. Thought gains direction by its self-reflection on its role with the Other. In this way the *eidos* connects to *telos*.

The Socratic Concept of the Work as Normative

The final embodiment of the freedom of human reason as lawgiver is the work (*das Werk*). The work is the basis of human culture and the basis of philosophy, whose task is to be the watchman of the ideal of freedom. Philosophy's theoretical task that underlies its role as custodian of the *telos* of freedom is the comprehension of culture as a synthesis of the diversity of symbolic forms, its grasp of the inner form of the human spirit.

Cassirer characterizes theories of knowledge in terms of three basis phenomena. He regards Bergson, Descartes, and Husserl as examples of the first basis phenomenon of the I or the monad. He says, "they are all directed toward the same point (the pure 'intuition' of the I), but they attain it in completely different ways."[18] Cassirer's aim is a philosophy of

18. Ibid., 172.

self-knowledge and he rejects the view that either introspection or pure intuition of the I can produce an adequate form of self-knowledge.

Cassirer says that the clearest example of a philosopher of the second basis phenomenon is Fichte. This requires us to see beyond the traditional interpretation of his philosophy as a doctrine of the pure ego. Fichte takes neither Descartes' nor Husserl's *cogito* as a starting point, instead he takes Kant's doctrine of "transcendental apperception." He shifts this doctrine from a logical to an ethical form, from the intellect to the will. The "I" for Fichte cannot be "shown" phenomenologically as a static entity. It can only be demonstrated through a *Tathandlung*. Cassirer says for Fichte "the I finds neither itself not the 'world' receptively as a simple datum. It 'posits' the world and posits itself in an originary, spontaneous act."[19] The I can be explained only in terms of an original drive to action per se, a drive not toward any object or goal but to action in general. The I on Fichte's view cannot be explained theoretically; it can be explained only practically, that is, in terms of a moral compulsion through which the Other and the world force themselves upon us.

Socrates is the central example of the philosophical standpoint of the third basis phenomenon of the work. When we move from the sphere of intuition, to the sphere of action, to that of contemplation we naturally move to Socratic philosophy. "In the history of philosophy it is Socrates who discovers this sphere, who puts it forth and establishes it as a central object for philosophical investigation and 'marvel.'"[20] Socrates contains, in his own figure as a philosopher, the two sides of philosophy—the basic opposition between theory and practice. Regarded in one way, especially as he is portrayed by Plato, Socrates is the artist of reason, the master of conceptual analysis, the discoverer of the logos.

Regarded in another way, as he is portrayed by Xenophon, Socrates is a moralist, the advocate of practical wisdom, although Plato also shows this side of Socrates. Cassirer says Socrates defies every attempt to "pin him down." This paradoxical status of Socrates' character is the basis of Socratic irony. Socrates not only employs irony as a type of philosophical thought but is himself an ironic figure, passing back and forth between these two positions. He is an ironic figure in the sense that irony as a trope is used to mean the opposite of what is literally said. Thus when Socrates makes

---

19. Ibid., 181–82.
20. Ibid., 184.

a theoretical assertion it often implies not just what is said but a practical meaning, and the reverse.

Socrates bases his philosophy of contemplation on the dictum of the Delphic Oracle: Know thyself. Cassirer says: "He does not call for 'self-knowledge' in the sense of some pure (monadic) looking inward (introspection, intuition of the I in the pure act of the *cogito*); instead, it means something completely new and unique for him. This call now means: know your *work* and know 'yourself' in your work; know what you do, so you can know what you know."[21] Cassirer points out that Socratic questioning starts not from a theoretical issue but from something occurring in the world of action. Socrates begins his questioning from something done by craftsmen, from a common view, or from a given human action. He proceeds from this toward a theoretical understanding of the elements involved.

Philosophical self-knowledge originates in the movement undertaken between the practical and the theoretical. Philosophy as grounded in the work has as its aim self-knowledge. Self-knowledge is the work that is made in dialogic speech. This form of contemplation takes the self out of itself because what is made in this activity has an "objectivity" that endures and is open to examination by others. Cassirer says that, unlike Platonic philosophy, the philosophy of symbolic forms does not take such speech in the direction of a pure realm of forms. Instead the philosophy of symbolic forms does not separate form from the work of culture. The work of philosophy is the illumination of the harmony in the diversity of culture.

In *The Logic of the Cultural Sciences*, Cassirer describes Vico in terms that place him along with Socrates as a philosopher of the third basis phenomenon. Where thought must choose between piecemeal knowledge of nature or piecemeal knowledge of subjective concepts, Cassirer claims Vico turns to the notion of works to satisfy both conditions. Cassirer says: "The works of human *culture* are the only ones that unite in themselves both conditions in which perfect knowledge is based; they have not only a conceptually apprehended existence but also a thoroughly determined, individual and historic one. However, the internal structure of this existence is accessible and open to the human spirit only because it is its creator."[22] Knowledge of works is the goal of philosophy for Vico because knowledge of works is identical to self-knowledge. This view of self-knowledge links

---

21. Ibid., 185–86.
22. Cassirer, *Cultural Sciences*, 9.

Vico to Socrates. "According to Vico, the real goal of our knowledge is not the knowledge of nature but human self-knowledge."[23]

Cassirer's turn to Socrates as the prime example of the third basis phenomenon allows him to look back on critical idealism and absolute idealism from a third standpoint. His method is not Kantian critique as such, nor is it Hegelian system. Cassirer's concept of "systematic review," which he mentions several times in various formulations but does not explain, is a version of Socratic questioning.[24] Systematic review is critical in the sense that it applies the question to what already exists in human culture. In this sense it is a "review," an "overview" (*Überblick*). It is also dialectical in the sense that its aim is to elicit the coherence of spirit to which the particular subject of its investigation is connected.

To accomplish this mode of philosophical thought, Cassirer requires an Archimedean point on which to stand that is neither transcendental nor absolute. It is not transcendental because Cassirer's intention is to grasp the inner form of the part of culture that is under question, not simply to state the conditions of its possibility from a point of view outside it. It is not absolute because, although Cassirer holds the true to be the whole, he is never actually at the point of the whole. Systematic review is a form of idealism that locates the act of philosophizing *in medias res*. Begin at any point in human experience and the philosophy of symbolic forms can connect to any other point through its perspective of the whole and say how, in specific terms, it falls within the logic or "tonality" of certain symbolic forms. This is a Socratic way of proceeding. The *agora* in Cassirer's case is the universality of cultural life, governed by the distinctively human power of the symbol.

For Cassirer, this ability to speak about culture is the key to human freedom because it allows us to think beyond the present moment—the immediacy that life produces or the action in which the will is presently engaged. The idea gives us access to the ideal and the ideal frees us from the immediate. Cassirer's standpoint is Socratic but less agile than that of Socrates. Socrates seems to move with ease between the theoretical and the practical, thinking easily within the *agora*, pushing those with whom he speaks toward the full-blooded sense of ideas. Cassirer is always the Olympian, struggling to escape the theoretical, to put forth its normative dimension, never fully able to let his philosophy move away from its scholarly

---

23. Ibid., 10.

24. Cassirer, *Philosophy of Symbolic Forms*, 4:56, 167, 227. See also Cassirer, *Problem of Knowledge*, 19.

basis. Cassirer comes closest to such moments in his later works, especially in his metaphysics of symbolic forms. Despite these constrictions, the decency of Cassirer's spirit, his insistence on the civility of culture, on the human as able to make the human ideal, produces philosophical morale in the face of the fragmentation of modern life and its philosophies of alienation and existence.

Human Culture as the Moral Education of the Self

Cassirer begins *An Essay on Man* with the sentence "That self-knowledge is the highest aim of philosophical inquiry appears to be generally acknowledged." He says that even the skeptic endorses the aim of self-knowledge: "We must try to break the chain connecting us with the outer world in order to enjoy our true freedom. 'La plus grande chose du monde c'est de scavoir être à soy,' writes Montaigne."[25] *An Essay on Man* is Cassirer's reflection on his Kantian-Hegelian-based statement of his philosophy of symbolic forms as it originally appeared in the 1920s. In *An Essay on Man* he announces the Socratic intent of his philosophy of culture and its connection with the question of human freedom.

Cassirer does not intend to replace his *Philosophy of Symbolic Forms* with this new work. In fact, in *An Essay on Man* he refers the reader back to the earlier work for a closer discussion and analysis of the technical problems involved. In this new work he is putting the old themes in a new light. The Socratic sense of his conception of symbolic forms is meant to add a new dimension to its sources in Kant and Hegel, not to replace these sources.

Cassirer takes his title from Alexander Pope's philosophical poem of 1732–34. What is Cassirer's intention in employing this title? He gives no specific explanation of it. Pope's poem has as its purpose to vindicate the ways of God to man and to prove that the order of the world is the best of all possible orders, that despite the appearance of evil there is a perfection of the whole that our limited vision often fails to see. This seems like Voltaire's satire on Leibniz's metaphysics, and indeed, Samuel Johnson said that Pope's attempt to show that "whatever is, is right" reminds us of Pangloss's views in *Candide*. This is not Cassirer's purpose in his *Essay*. Cassirer's aim is probably to point to Pope's dictum that the "proper study of mankind is

---

25. Cassirer, *Essay on Man*, 1.

man" and to remind us that the Enlightenment contains a resolute humanism that is still valuable.[26] In his *Philosophy of the Enlightenment* Cassirer says that this work, together with *The Platonic Renaissance in England* and *The Individual and the Cosmos in Renaissance Philosophy*, constitute a "phenomenology of the philosophic spirit."[27] This phenomenology shows that human beings are the makers of the human world of culture.

Cassirer's critique of modernity rests on the breakdown of a common context that can support the quest for self-knowledge. The "crisis in man's knowledge of himself," as Cassirer calls it, is based on the modern fragmentation of knowledge, which is also a fragmentation of the human self. What the human being is, is understood in terms of the primary intent of the field conducting investigation into the human. In such approaches, the human is reduced to any one of its aspects, to sexual instinct, economic drive, emotional reactions, class interests, or biological conditions. Cassirer says, "Theologians, scientists, politicians, sociologists, biologists, psychologists, ethnologists, economists all approached the problem from their own viewpoints. To combine or unify all these particular aspects and perspectives was impossible."[28]

At the basis of Cassirer's concern is the Socratic question: What is man? Cassirer says: "Only one question remains: What is man? Socrates always maintains and defends the ideal of an objective, absolute, universal truth. But the only universe he knows, and to which all his inquiries refer, is the universe of man. His philosophy—if he possesses a philosophy—is strictly anthropological."[29] He regards the "clue to the nature of man" to be the symbol. As mentioned earlier, he defines man as *animal symbolicum*. Following the method of Socrates in the *Republic*, Cassirer sees the nature of the individual writ large in the forms of human culture. If Cassirer can show that all cultural activities are various ways of forming the world through the power of the symbol, the individual will encounter its own nature writ large in culture. The human being will understand itself as an organism distinguished from other organisms by its unique power of symbolic formation. The symbol will provide the key to a functional account of human nature, one that allows the human being to understand itself through its work (*Werk*).

26. Cassirer, *Philosophy of the Enlightenment*, 5.
27. Ibid., vi.
28. Cassirer, *Essay on Man*, 21.
29. Ibid., 4.

Moral Philosophy and Culture

Cassirer sees this functional conception of human nature as an extension of the Socratic conception of man as a creature that is always in search for itself. Such a creature is by its nature involved in the examination of its life. In Socrates Cassirer sees reason as connected to the human aim to be human. Cassirer says that for Socrates the human individual is that being who is capable of asking a rational question and giving a rational answer. He says: "Both his knowledge and his morality are comprehended in this circle. It is by this fundamental faculty, by this faculty of giving a response to himself and to others, that man becomes a 'responsible' being, a moral subject."[30]

Here Cassirer suggests a positive way to view the irony of the figure of Socrates that he describes in the *Metaphysics of Symbolic Forms*, that when we regard Socrates at one moment he is the theoretician and at another he appears as the moralist. Socrates, as said above, passes freely between these two approaches to the world by the medium of the question. The device of the question allows the individual to make reason functional. Reason becomes the basis for both our response to the world and defining our responsibility in it. It is through reason that we move between theoretical and moral inquiry, and the medium of this rationality is the power both to respond to the world and to act on it through the formation of symbols. Cassirer expresses his commitment to Socratic philosophy as: "The Socratic problem and the Socratic method can never be forgotten or obliterated."[31]

Although in Cassirer's account we obtain a new version of the Socratic approach to philosophy, we do not obtain a doctrine of the individual. Once Cassirer adopts the method of the *Republic* to approach the nature of the individual writ large, he, unlike the Platonic Socrates, does not return to the small letters of the individual and offer an account of the virtues. It is here that his attachment to Socrates and his Kantianism come into conflict. Cassirer speaks only of the power of reason to form human ideals set against the purely animal world of reactions. Unlike other animals, the human animal can respond to the world in terms of "ought" or the ideal, which is made possible because of the freedom from immediacy achieved by the power of symbolic formation.

---

30. Ibid., 6.
31. Ibid.

Conclusion

At the end of *An Essay on Man*, having described the various forms of cultural life, Cassirer introduces two central ideas: harmony and self-liberation. The task of philosophy is to show the moral possibilities of a harmony of symbolic forms, which does not exist as such in cultural life, in which various forms struggle to dominate others. Philosophy can hold up to this the Heraclitean conception of "harmony in contrariety, as in the case of the bow and the lyre."[32] This is a fulfillment of Schweitzer's demand for the watchman. Because philosophy understands culture as a totality, philosophy can understand the imbalances in cultural life and pose the ideal of harmony against actual conflicts. Philosophy, which is not itself a symbolic form, as Cassirer says in one of the fragments related to his conception of the metaphysics of symbolic forms,[33] has the ability and the duty to show theoretically the harmony in the contraries of the symbolic forms that make up culture.

Philosophy can also show the connection of culture to human freedom. Cassirer says: "Human culture taken as a whole may be described as the process of man's progressive self-liberation. Language, art, religion, science, are various phases in this process. In all of them man discovers and proves a new power—the power to build up a world of his own, an 'ideal' world. Philosophy cannot give up its search for a fundamental unity in this ideal world."[34] This echoes what Cassirer finds in Kant and Hegel, that freedom is tied to the process of civilization. Self-knowledge allows the self to free itself from its own immediacy and in the distance from the immediate the basis for its freedom, its self-liberation, is formed. The self becomes the maker of itself and knows itself in its work. The self's power to make its own being in its own distinctive activity of reason gives it a moral self, for it is responsible for its world, as it is the maker of it.

---

32. Ibid., 222–23, 228.
33. Cassirer, *Philosophy of Symbolic Forms*, 4:226.
34. Cassirer, *Essay on Man*, 228.

2

Culture and History

Philosophy of History

As expressed in the previous chapter, culture is always normative for the individual. As the individual absorbs the forms of human culture through education, the individual acquires a vital sense of what it means to be human. In this way, education is in essence moral and the philosophy of culture is also the philosophy of human education. By acquiring culture the individual does not simply acquire knowledge, the individual also acquires a way to act, a way to be human. To live in history and to understand oneself as part of history is distinctive to human existence. Moral philosophy requires a sense of history in order to provide moral reasoning with context. Human culture exists in history and to formulate a philosophy of culture is also to adhere explicitly or implicitly to a view of the nature of history.

In the four volumes of the *Philosophy of Symbolic Forms*, Cassirer says little of history as a symbolic form. His most substantial remarks are in the second volume on *Mythical Thought*. He contrasts mythical time in which the past, present, and future exist on a single plane with historical time, which originates in the internal differentiations of genealogy and chronology.[1] Throughout the works of his systematic philosophy Cassirer frequently mentions the triad of myth, religion, and art. At times he alters this list to include language, the subject of the first volume of the *Philosophy of Symbolic Forms*, but he does not include history.

A discussion of history as a symbolic form does not occur in Cassirer's published works until *An Essay on Man*, various aspects of which have been discussed in the previous chapter. Cassirer wrote this work in response to the urging of his English and American friends that he publish a translation

---

1. Cassirer, *Philosophy of Symbolic Forms*, 2:104–40.

of the *Philosophy of Symbolic Forms*. The welcome surprise to readers of this work was not only lively chapters written in English on myth and religion, language, and science but the appearance of equally full chapters on art and history. Much of Cassirer's conception of art became well-known through the works of Susanne Langer.[2] Some general analysis has been done of Cassirer's views of history but no detailed attention has been given to Vico as a fundamental source of these views. This most historical of modern philosophers and author of seminal works on the history of the problem of knowledge, the Renaissance, and the Enlightenment has a unique conception of the philosophy of history most directly expressed in his final lecture to the 1941 Yale seminar that reaches a fuller statement in his chapter on history in *An Essay on Man*.

What are the principles of Cassirer's philosophy of history and hence perhaps of the philosophy of history itself? What are their sources? What place does history occupy within his general system of symbolic forms? In a short space it is not possible to develop full answers to these fundamental questions, but it is possible at least to suggest their outlines. An account of history as a symbolic form must begin from what Cassirer means in general by the idea of "symbolic form," an idea that was broached in the previous chapter.

For Cassirer the medium of human reason that defines human nature is the symbol. All of human experience, culture, and thought occur through the symbol. There is no distinctively human activity for Cassirer that is non-symbolic. The distinction between the literal and the symbolic for Cassirer is a distinction between types of symbolization. To designate one level of meaning as literal is in fact to affirm one type of symbolic formation over another. For example to regard the representational grasp of the object as literal and its aesthetic formation as symbolic is to contrast one form of symbolization with another. This contrast is between language used referentially in relation to the object and language used presentationally to capture the object's significance for human subjectivity, grasping the object as a medium of feeling and emotion.

Cassirer says: "Under a 'symbolic form' should be understood each energy of spirit [*Geist*] through which a spiritual [*geistig*] content or meaning is connected with a concrete, sensory sign and is internally adapted to this sign."[3] A symbol is an inseparable bond between the "spiritual" (*geis-*

---

2. Langer, *Philosophical Sketches*, 56.
3. Cassirer, "Der Begriff," 175.

tig) and the sensible (*sinnlich*). A symbol is something physical, a mark on a surface or a breath of wind, which also conveys something non-physical, a meaning. Cassirer's conception of the symbol is rooted in his conception of "symbolic pregnance" (*symbolische Prägnanz*). Cassirer says: "By symbolic pregnance we mean the way in which a perception as a sensory experience contains at the same time a certain nonintuitive meaning which it immediately and concretely represents."[4] Cassirer takes this term from the "law of pregnance" of Gestalt psychology, but the term "symbolic form" is distinctive to Cassirer's philosophy. Its source is twofold. One source is the Hegelian aesthetician Friedrich Theodor Vischer's use of "*das Symbol*" and "*der Symbolbegriff*" in his essay, "Das Symbol." The other source is Heinrich Hertz's conception of science, as dependent upon systems of symbols, in his *Principles of Mechanics*.[5] From these sources, Cassirer formulates the idea of the symbol as the key to all activities of human culture.

Cassirer demonstrates his conception of symbolic form in terms of a thought-experiment. He asks the reader to consider a *Linienzug*, a graph-like line drawing.[6] He says we may first regard the line as simply an expressive object displaying a tension in its shape and conveying a feeling of a certain sense of motion. We may then shift our perspective and regard the drawing as an object of theoretical significance, as depicting a mathematical proportion, as having a geometrical shape. We can pass back toward the expressive character of the line but now grasp it as a mythical-magical form, a sacred or profane sign. We may now gain new distance from the drawing and apprehend it as an aesthetic ornament, appreciating its purely visual qualities. Cassirer's point is that all of these ways of apprehending the object are writ large in the areas of human culture. Each of the forms of culture such as myth, religion, language, art, history, and science originate and are grounded in the various perspectives that can be taken on any object. Any one of these ways of directly apprehending the object is "symbolically pregnant" with the symbolic form that corresponds to it in the structure of human culture. The object itself is the harmony or systematic set of interrelations of all the perspectives on it. No one symbolic form reveals the

---

4. Cassirer, *Philosophy of Symbolic Forms*, 3:202.

5. Vischer, "Das Symbol," 169–73 and 192–93. On Hertz, see Cassirer, *Philosophy of Symbolic Forms*, 1:175.

6. Cassirer, *Philosophy of Symbolic Forms*, 3:200–201.

"real" object over the others. The "real" object is so to speak the sum of all its forms of apprehension.[7]

History

In the thought-experiment of the *Linienzug* Cassirer does not mention apprehending it as a historical object. But in his concluding remarks for a seminar in the philosophy of history he gave at Yale University, he formulates a similar example. He asks us to assume we are in the position of Robinson Crusoe abandoned on a desert island unable to detect any traces of human culture. Yet by chance we come upon a particular stone that attracts our attention such that we begin to study it to discover its nature. We may first, he says, be interested in its physical and chemical qualities. We may regard it from the point of view of a mineralogist or geologist. He then asks us to imagine that we suddenly notice some marks on the stone that appear to recur in a regular order. We now realize these may be written characters. We still perceive the stone as a physical object yet the characters on it take us from the stone as part of a mere world of things to the stone as part of a world of symbols. He concludes: "The physical marks have become significant signs. They begin to 'speak' to me. In my perfect seclusion from all human beings I suddenly hear the message of a human world."[8]

In *An Essay on Man* Cassirer says: "The historian, like the physicist, lives in a material world. Yet what he finds at the very beginning of his research is not a world of physical objects but a symbolic universe—a world of symbols." He claims that the object of historical understanding is part of human culture, something that has been made, that has a human stamp on it. The physicist comes to his object as something natural, not a product of human ingenuity or purpose. Cassirer concludes: "Not things or events but documents or monuments are the first and immediate objects of our historical knowledge."[9]

Cassirer regards this distinction between natural objects and historical or cultural objects as obvious but says it is curious that the fundamentally symbolic character of the object of historical thought has been overlooked by modern discussions of historical method. He says: "Most writers looked for the difference between history and science in the *logic*, not in the *object*

---

7. Ibid., 1:105–14.
8. Cassirer, *Symbol, Myth, and Culture,* 136.
9. Cassirer, *Essay on Man,* 175.

of history."[10] Cassirer says there is no special logic of historical thought. The historian like the scientist must employ the same general laws of thought. The historian and the scientist are bound to the same standards of reasoning and argument, of inductive inferences and investigation of causes. Logical rules govern thought in a constant manner in all areas of inquiry.

Although Cassirer regards the general principles of logic to be required for all forms of knowledge, the way in which investigation is conducted in history differs from that of the biological and physical sciences. Cassirer proposes three terms as keys to distinguishing between these: *explanation*, *description*, and *interpretation*.[11] He regards the physical sciences as directed toward *explaining* natural phenomena in terms of causal laws. Cassirer has in mind Kant's determinate judgments in which a particular is subsumed under a general rule. In *Substance and Function* and in the third volume of the *Philosophy of Symbolic Forms* Cassirer has transformed Kant's theory of the determinate judgment into his conception of the functional concept that is mathematical in form and is at the basis of modern science.[12] Cassirer regards the biological sciences as based on the idea of organic form and its counterpart in Kant's critical philosophy of reflective judgments. Such judgments are essentially *descriptive* of phenomena. They reflect the ways in which organic life is a system of wholes, the sense in which the whole is a law of its "parts." It is not my purpose here in these limited remarks to discuss the full features and problems of these aspects of Cassirer's epistemology and philosophy of science. I only wish as does Cassirer in his discussions of history to separate them off from the sense of *interpretation* that is fundamental to historical thought.

Cassirer holds that in history just as much as in the various sciences we desire to know the causes of things. He claims that in every historical causation there is something more than physical and biological causation. He says: "There is not only causation in general but there is what we call 'motivation.' Of course 'motivation' is by no means opposed to causality; it is a special form of causality."[13] His example is Caesar crossing The Rubicon. After the historian has considered all the factors that can be said to contribute to this event, the historian must consider in addition the "personality" of Caesar, in which is rooted his "motivation." Cassirer does

---

10. Ibid.
11. Cassirer, *Symbol, Myth, and Culture*, 130.
12. Cassirer, *Substance and Function*, chap. 1; *Philosophy of Symbolic Forms*, 3:pt.3.
13. Cassirer, *Symbol, Myth, and Culture*, 128.

not intend this in a psychological sense. It is not his intention to reduce historical analysis to psychological analysis. He claims that the historian must seek to "understand" Caesar. This is an example, Cassirer says, of what he means by *interpretation*. He intends the English term so used to be the equivalent of the German *"historisches Verstehen."*[14] To interpret Caesar and his crossing of The Rubicon the historian, Cassirer claims, must *resurrect* Caesar as a historical character and the totality of the period of Roman civilization in which he lived.

Cassirer says that history is recollection. It is not simply memory, not simply the recalling of past events and agents. As recollection history involves ordering the past so that earlier phases of it are grasped as generating later phases. But when something occurs at a given time in history there is always more in it than what has preceded it. In investigating the physical facts upon which an account of the past is formulated the historian employs all the available means provided by the natural sciences. But the historian's aim is not merely to establish a definite chronological order based on the artifacts of a past age. The historian moves from a recollection of the past to its resurrection: to bring the past back to life. Cassirer's term for this is "palingenesis." Cassirer says the historian "cannot think or speak without using general terms. But he infuses into his concepts and words his own inner feelings, and thus gives them a new sound and a new color—the color of a personal life."[15]

Cassirer stands squarely against Ranke's conception of the aim of history to efface everything personal on the part of the historian and to present only what actually happened. Yet Cassirer speaks very highly of Ranke's actual writings on history. He does not find Ranke to follow the view that Ranke theoretically advocates to present the past *wie es eigentlich gewesen war* ("as it actually was"). For the historian to efface his or her personal life, Cassirer claims, would not be to achieve a higher objectivity. It would be to cut off the source necessary to all true historical thought. He says: "If I put out the light of my own personal experience I cannot see and I cannot judge of the experience of others."[16] Cassirer regards history as dependent on the imagination of the artist. Elements of the symbolic form of art enter into that of history. But unlike the artist the historian cannot allow his or her imagination to produce fiction. This freedom of the artist is closed to

14. Ibid., 129.
15. Cassirer, *Essay on Man*, 187.
16. Ibid.

the historian. History is a combination of scientific inquiry to establish the facts of the past and artistic imagination to recreate the senses of culture and human life that revolved around those facts. This combination when successfully achieved results in "interpretation" or "historical understanding" (*historisches Verstehen*).

The historian is an artist but Cassirer quoting Schiller says, "there is an art of passion, but there cannot be a 'passionate art.'"[17] Art as well as history requires distance from its subject. A work of art cannot be simply the embodiment or product of passion. "History" Cassirer says, "is a history of passions; but if history itself attempts to be passionate it ceases to be history."[18] In the historian's resurrection of the past, the past is given theoretical form, not simply personal form. Ultimately Cassirer claims history "is a form of self-knowledge. . . . In history man constantly returns to himself; he attempts to recollect and actualize the whole of his past experience."[19] This historical self is not an individual self. Cassirer begins *An Essay on Man* with the statement that the highest aim of philosophical inquiry is self-knowledge.[20] Thus his discussion of history as a symbolic form culminates in history as self-knowledge.

Cassirer places history very close to philosophy. For the Platonic-Socrates the basis of self-knowledge is the recollection of the eternal forms outside of time. For Cassirer the basis of self-knowledge is the recollection of the symbolic forms of human culture as they develop in time. Attention to history is the crucial factor by which Cassirer wishes to move from a substance-based conception of human nature to a functional conception of the human. Human beings make their world through their systems of symbols and they are what they make. To recollect and resurrect culture historically and then to comprehend it philosophically is to understand human nature.

Cassirer criticizes Windelband's view that science is nomothetic but that history is idiographic, that it deals not with general laws but with particular facts, a view that became the basis of Rickert's claim that to regard empirical reality as nature is to regard it as universal. But to regard it as history is to attend to the particular. Dilthey's view that the object of history is the individual is close to this. Cassirer rejects these approaches that

17. Ibid., 190.
18. Ibid., 191.
19. Ibid.
20. Ibid., 1.

see history as a type of investigation that focuses on the particular or the individual rather than the universal. History like all forms of investigation involves a union of the particular and the universal. But history has its own way of making this connection. Hippolyte Taine holds that like the scientist, the historian seeks to discover both the facts and their causes. But Cassirer claims that Taine overlooks the point that the facts are not immediately given to the historian. They are not observable like physical or chemical facts. Historical facts must be reconstructed. No amount of the scientific application of the laws of nature to human actions and productions will allow us to penetrate the uniquely symbolic universe that is human culture. Cassirer says: "The category of meaning is not to be reduced to the category of being."[21]

Cassirer claims that history might be regarded not as a branch of physics but as a branch of semantics. By this classification Cassirer means that history is part of the general study of the principles of the interrelation of signs and symbols and the senses in which these are keys to the nature of the human world. Thus Cassirer says: "What we seek in history is not the knowledge of an external thing but a knowledge of ourselves."[22] Cassirer holds that despite the theories of history as advanced by historians such as Taine, in their actual practice of writing history they follow his description of historical method. The one historian Cassirer points to who most fulfills his view is Jakob Burckhardt whose work on Constantine the Great and on the Renaissance are self-conscious reconstructions of the past. Burckhardt held that history requires the power of imagination to fill in the gaps of observations, that the history of a given period requires the talent of the artist to synthesize and present as a whole the facts and their causal relationships that can be scientifically and empirically adduced.

New Science of Ideal Eternal History

To understand ourselves as human agents and hence as moral agents, we must understand the nature of history. We may gain further insight into this relationship by considering Cassirer's sources of his philosophy of history. In *The Myth of the State* Cassirer says, "Thucydides was the first to attack the mythical conception of history. The elimination of the 'fabulous'

---

21. Ibid., 195.
22. Ibid., 203.

was one of his first and principal concerns."[23] This view of Thucydides as the beginning of a truly historical way of thinking is also to be found in Cassirer's remarks in the earlier Yale seminar on the philosophy of history. All symbolic forms begin in and arise from a base in mythical thought. History is no exception. In beginning his second volume of the *Philosophy of Symbolic Forms* devoted to the nature of mythical thought Cassirer says that Vico was the founder of "a completely new philosophy of mythology."[24] Later in the fourth volume of *The Problem of Knowledge* Cassirer says Vico is "the real discoverer of the myth."[25] In *An Essay on Man* Cassirer attributes the founding of the philosophy of history to Vico. He says that "historical consciousness" is a very late product of human civilization not found before the Greeks and even with the Greeks we do not find analysis of history as a particular form of thought. Cassirer says: "Such an analysis did not appear until the eighteenth century. The concept of history first reaches maturity in the work of Vico and Herder."[26]

It is not accidental that Vico is the founder of the modern philosophy of mythology as well as the founder of the modern philosophy of history. The one requires the other. Thucydides and the Greek historians can turn from the fabulous accounts of human events to their historical narration but this is not accompanied by a philosophy of mythical thought involving comprehension of the internal logic of the mythical formation of events. Plato divides philosophical truth from the productions of the poets in the ancient quarrel with the poets of the tenth book of the *Republic* and in his arguments with poetry in other dialogues such as *Ion*. Philosophical truth depends upon the *eidos* not the *eikōn* of the poets. Vico transposes the terms of their quarrel into a new form with his doctrine of "poetic wisdom" (*sapienza poetica*). Poetic wisdom is the basis of Vico's philosophy of mythology. Vico conceives the myths preserved by the ancient Greek poets to be a complete form of thought (in Cassirer's terms a symbolic form). Myths are not the results of errors and illusions about the real nature of things. They are products of a way of ordering the world that follows the principles of imagination (*fantasia*) rather than of cognition.

At the heart of Vico's conception of mythical or poetic wisdom is the "imaginative universal" (*universale fantastico*). The imagination relies on

23. Cassirer, *Myth of the State*, 53.
24. Cassirer, *Philosophy of Symbolic Forms*, 2:3.
25. Cassirer, *Problem of Knowledge*, 296.
26. Cassirer, *Essay on Man*, 172–73.

"poetic characters' (*caratteri poetici*) as its way of forming experience. A poetic character, a god or a hero such as Jove or Juno, Achilles or Odysseus is at once a particular figure and a universal, a kind of "actual ideal." The mythic mind is unable to form the abstract concept "courage" and predicate it of various individuals who could be claimed to possess this virtue. Instead the mythic mind grasps "courage" as having the form of the "poetic character" or hero Achilles and univocally predicates "Achilles" of various individuals. Achilles is literally one and many at once. The ease with which mythical thinking can join diverse persons, things, and events together as one gives it the logic of a dream. It is as difficult as is a dream for cognitive thought to penetrate.

Vico's philosophy of myth allows him to formulate the philosophy of history because he regards myths as the first histories. A myth is a true story, *vera narratio*, in that it states a truth that can only be reached by the imagination. Myths are the original acts of the imagination through which the life of nations is formed. Cassirer says that Vico's great discovery was that "the first nations did not think by concepts; they thought in poetic images, they spoke in fables and wrote in hieroglyphics."[27] The myths state in imaginative form the truths upon which any nation is founded. Once a nation has developed past its origins in mythical thought and life to a level of cognitive knowledge and life, imagination is required to recover its origins. The historian, like the artist, must draw on the imagination to attempt to recover something of its originating power to produce their respective forms of thought. The historian must go to school with the poets not only to recollect the origin of the life of nations but to develop the power of imagination necessary to the art of re-creation. The historian's unique contribution to human culture is the resurrection of its past in thought.

Vico's *New Science* depends upon two great methodological principles that underlie Cassirer's philosophy of history, although Cassirer does not in his discussions of history explicitly acknowledge these as his sources. The first of these is Vico's famous principle that "the true is the made" (*verum esse ipsum factum*).[28] In his remarks on Vico in his Yale seminar Cassirer discusses this principle as crucial to Vico's thought but he does not explicitly connect it to his own. This principle that the true is made underlies Cassirer's claim that the object of history is different from the object of natural science. Vico claims that our knowledge of nature is a kind of conscious-

---

27. Cassirer, *Symbol, Myth, and Culture*, 107.
28. Vico, *Ancient Wisdom*, 45–46.

ness (*coscienza*) because we do not make natural objects. As Cassirer says the objects investigated by the natural sciences are external to the human world. Nature is what surrounds the human world and what determines the conditions under which the human world develops and realizes itself. Vico claims that our knowledge of the civil world or culture is different in kind from our knowledge of nature because what is known in the human world of culture is something already made by humans.

Cassirer's way of saying this is that the object of the historian is already "symbolic," the product of the human power to symbolize. Vico claims we can have a science (*scienza*) of the human world because in principle we can know what we make. The objects of cultural or historical investigation that we wish to know are extensions of ourselves. By taking them up as objects of thought we come to know ourselves. This kind of knowledge is self-knowledge. Vico first realized this principle by a consideration of mathematical thought in which he saw that the truths of mathematics are such because we make them from the general principle of mathematics. In the *New Science* he applied the same reasoning to the nature of history.

The second principle is Vico's "new critical art" (*nuova arte critica*). This is based on the joining together of philosophy and philology. Vico claims that philosophy through reason aims at formulating what is true in universal terms. Philology through its attention to the particulars of the languages, customs, laws and deeds of any given nation aims at the certain. These are certain in that they are the facts of a nation's life, that is, the particular words and meanings of its language, its specific customs, its positive laws, and deeds of its political and social life. Only when these certains (*certi*) are brought together with the trues (*veri*) of reason do we have a full knowledge of human history. Vico's philosophical-philological method that guides his new critical art is parallel to Cassirer's claim that historical knowledge is neither based on universals nor on particulars but on the bond between them. These two factors, the philosophical and the philological, are brought together in Vico's new critical art by means of imagination.

Vico through his doctrine of *corso e ricorso* in which the life of any nation exists in a three-fold cycle—of an age of gods, in which the world is formed in terms of gods, an age of heroes, in which social order depends upon the embodiment of values in the figures of heroes, and an age of humans in which the world is made intelligible through reason and written laws—sees culture itself as a continual act of resurrection. The Vichian new scientist portrays this process in terms that are ultimately imaginative and poetic. Vico's understanding of historical knowledge is thus very close to that which Cassirer most admires in Burckhardt that history has ultimately the character of poetic composition. But for Cassirer as for Vico, this composition must have within it both the logical and causal ordering of events established by philosophical reasoning and the factual certainties established by philological analysis.

As mentioned earlier Cassirer regards Herder as the continuation of the approach to history that begins in Vico's *New Science*. Vico's opponent is Descartes whose conception of knowledge as Cassirer points out excludes history as well as all works of the imagination from the rational pursuit of truth. Cassirer rightly says: "In the philosophy of Descartes history has no place."[29] He also says: "In a certain sense we may regard the introduction to Vico's works as a new *Discours de la méthode*—applied to history, instead of mathematics or physics."[30] As Descartes is the founder of the modern conception of scientific method so Vico is the founder of the modern conception of historical method.

Cassirer's connection of Vico and Herder precedes the major study in Vichian literature of Isaiah Berlin's *Vico and Herder*. Herder knew of Vico before writing his *Ideas toward the Philosophy of the History of Mankind* (1784–87), but Herder first discusses Vico in his *Letters in Furtherance of Humanity* (1797).[31] Berlin understands Herder as a part of the counter-Enlightenment, the main figures of which he regards as Vico, Herder, and Hamann. Cassirer also sees Herder's approach to history as counter to the Enlightenment ideal that regards all former ages as in the dark and all history developing toward the perfection of the age of Enlightenment. Herder, Cassirer says, saw the content of humanity as distributed in history into a thousand shapes through all parts of the world and through all countries: "Every age and every nation has its perfections and imperfections, its advantages and its defects."[32] Herder's vision is thus in sharp contrast to Voltaire's approach to history in which the only ages to be studied are those that achieve a level of perfection, all in between is of no significance.

Cassirer claims that Herder does not completely abandon the Enlightenment ideal of a teleology of history but it undergoes a substantial change

29. Cassirer, *Symbol, Myth, and Culture*, 96.
30. Ibid., 103.
31. Fisch, "Introduction," *Autobiography of Giambattista Vico*, 68.
32. Cassirer, Lecture on Herder to the Yale seminar on the "Philosophy of History," ms. p. 11.

in the thought of Herder. According to Herder there is not a rectilinear progress in history toward a realm of ends. For Herder we cannot isolate ends from means. Cassirer says: "Every event in history must at the same time be regarded as a means and as an end."[33] This end does not exist beyond the course of the event. All in history has a meaning that is realized in its own terms and must be understood as such. Cassirer holds that on the one hand this approach of Herder is influenced by Rousseau's conception of education and his *Discourses*, and on the other it has a source in the metaphysics of Leibniz's *Monadology*. Herder's views are close to Rousseau's conception that childhood cannot be regarded as a mere means to adulthood. It has its own worth such that the individual must be educated not by external means but by the conditions of the child's own human development. It is also close to Rousseau's thesis that we can only understand humanity by understanding its origins and that from these origins there is no evidence that there has been real moral progress.

Considered in metaphysical rather than moral terms Cassirer sees Leibniz's conception of the monad as providing the groundwork for Herder's conception of history. In his doctrine of the monad Leibniz has transposed substance from a static to a dynamic principle. The monad is a self-developing reality, a dynamical being that has its own internal causation. This is parallel to Herder's and Vico's conceptions of a nation. Leibniz's doctrine of individuation in which no two things are exactly alike (the identity of indiscernibles) is parallel to Herder's and Vico's view that each nation has its own life yet is part of the total history of humanity. In Cassirer's philosophy of symbolic forms these ideas of Leibniz are present.

Each symbolic form has its own inner form, its own manner of development. Each is individuated from the others yet has a place within the totality of human culture in which each symbolic form is alive. History's task is to resurrect the past in all its unique forms and developments. The source of Cassirer's use of "palingenesis" as the term for this task is Goethe's statement in a letter written in 1772 shortly after his first meeting with Herder. In this letter Cassirer says: "Goethe speaks enthusiastically of Herder's power of 'Palingenesis'—of his incomparable gift to regenerate the life of past times."[34] From Vico Cassirer takes his principle that history differs from science in terms of its object (the true is the made) and his principle that historical thinking depends on both the universal and particular (the

---

33. Ibid., ms., pp.12–13.
34. Ibid., ms., p.8.

union of the philosophical and philological in Vico's new critical art). From Herder he adds to this his principle of palingenesis.

Nature and Culture

A final question to be considered is where history may fit in the overall scheme of knowledge that is implicit in Cassirer's conception of human culture. In his first published work, *Leibniz' System in seinen wissenschaftlichen Grundlagen* (1902), Cassirer inserts some brief remarks on the sense in which Vico is the founder of the *Geisteswissenschaften*.[35] Cassirer says that the modern foundation of the *Naturwissenschaften* derives from Descartes and Leibniz but Vico is the unique source for the origin of the *Geisteswissenschaften*. Cassirer holds this view of Vico throughout his career, making special use of it in his late work *The Logic of the Cultural Sciences* (1942).[36] The distinction between the *Natur-* and the *Geisteswissenschaften* is central to the problem of knowledge as approached by the various schools of neo-Kantianism at the turn of the twentieth century. Although Cassirer's development of a critique of culture from the critique of reason takes his philosophy well beyond its roots in the Marburg school of Cohen and Natorp, the distinction between the natural and the cultural forms of knowledge remains central to it.

Geist for Cassirer is a metaphysical principle. *Kultur* is the epistemological principle that corresponds to it. *Kultur* refers to the way in which *Geist* distinctively underlies human activity. The forms of cultural life that are made by man as *animal symbolicum* are inherently forms of knowledge. The symbolic forms are ways of living in the world and they are also at once ways of knowing the world. These actual ways of knowing and living become the subjects of theoretical thought once purely cognitive ways of grasping experience have developed in human culture.

Conceptual thought per se occurs once the human spirit has gained sufficient distance from the immediate presence of the object. Concepts can be formed when consciousness passes beyond the immediacy of the mythical image and beyond the linguistic representation of the world of things. Nature-concepts (*Naturbegriffe*) upon which the natural sciences depend are determinate in form, that is, such concepts are universals and able to subsume the particular in an unambiguous way under them.

---

35. Cassirer, *Leibniz' System*, 447–49.
36. See Verene, "Vico's Influence on Cassirer," 105–11.

Cassirer explains this logic of nature-concepts through an example of the concept "gold." He says, "Thus a determined empirically existing substance, a certain metal, can be subsumed under the concept *gold* if, and only if, it exhibits the relevant basic property and consequently all the other properties that can be derived from it."[37]

Cassirer says what we mean by gold is that which has a specific gravity, a specific electrical conductivity, a specific coefficient of expansion, etc. Underlying this explanation of nature-concepts is Cassirer's general interpretation of the functional concept signified as ø(x). In relation to this formula, (x) represents a specific series of coordinated properties of metals taken from established tables of weights, conductivity, expansion, etc. Gold as signified by ø is that which exactly has this combined set of properties. The universal ø and the particular (x) are held together in an inseparable bond. The idea of "gold" has no meaning apart from this order of specific properties and the properties individually have no meaning apart from their being properties of gold.

In relation to culture-concepts no such principles of determination and subsumption are possible. The cultural sciences base their theories on concepts of form and style. Cassirer's two most prominent examples of the use of such concepts are Heinrich Wölfflin's styles of the "linear" and the "painterly" as the organizing concepts in his *Principles of Art History* and Burckhardt's concept of the "Renaissance man" as distinguished from the "medieval man" in his *Culture of the Renaissance*. Cassirer says that the individual figures of the Renaissance can never be subsumed under the concept "Renaissance man" in the way "we subsume a body given here and now, a piece of metal, under the concept *gold* after finding that it fulfills all the conditions of gold known to us." Cassirer continues: "When we characterize Leonardo da Vinci and Aretino, Marsilio Ficino and Machiavelli, Michelangelo and Cesare Borgia as 'men of the renaissance,' we do not mean to say that there is to be found in them a definite individual feature that is fixed as regards its contents, in which they all agree."[38]

We cannot understand the meaning of these historical figures if approached singly as individuals, nor can we understand what the concept "Renaissance man" means on its own apart from seeing it in these figures. There is "a unity of *direction* [*Richtung*], not a unity of *being*" in such

---

37. Cassirer, *Cultural Sciences*, 70.
38. Ibid., 72.

style- and form-concepts.[39] These figures can be considered in terms of the extent to which they fully embody or tend to depart from the properties attached to the form of the Renaissance man; just as various artistic or literary works can be understood as to how much they instantiate the style of an epoch.

Although Cassirer does not explicitly claim so, his logic of the formation of culture-concepts is foreshadowed in Vico's logic of imaginative universals. At the level of mythical consciousness or "poetic wisdom" the figure of Achilles is predicated univocally of all courageous individuals, just as for the cognitive mind "courage" is predicated univocally of all such persons, as mentioned above. But as Vico says we cannot fully penetrate the mentality of the first humans who could think of universals literally as individuals and of individuals literally as universals. As Cassirer explains, for the mythic mind when the dancer puts on the mask of the god, the dancer literally *is* the god.[40] The dancer in no way is a representation of the god. The historical mind like the scientific mind is theoretical. Thus for the historical mind culture-concepts are ideals that organize epochs and individuals.

Conclusion

As Vico's principle claims, the fact that human beings make culture means that they can make a science of culture. For Cassirer the science of culture is the philosophy of culture, which is built from harmonizing the results of the various sciences of culture, the *Kulturwissenschaften*. For both Cassirer, and Vico in his own way, *Kuturwissenschaft* is historical in form. Its logic is that of culture-concepts. In the end for Cassirer the task of the philosopher is equipoise. As the human being stands between nature and culture, between what is and what is made, the philosopher in pursuit of the problem of knowledge stands between nature-concepts and culture-concepts, each requiring the other and neither reducing itself to the other.

History as a symbolic form occurs through a combination of the symbolic forms of science and art. On Cassirer's view historical thought requires joining the empirical investigation of facts with the power of the aesthetic imagination to produce a palingenesis of the past. This approach

---

39. Ibid.
40. Cassirer, *Philosophy of Symbolic Forms*, 2:39.

is first achieved by Vico's "new critical art" of joining philosophical with philological means of investigation to explain historical events.

Human education requires the individual to have a grasp of the origin of the human world. In its most fundamental sense, self-knowledge requires the individual to have an autobiography, to have the power to see that one has a personal history and that this history in some way recapitulates the history of humankind itself. It is not possible to grasp oneself as a moral being capable of moral development without a sense of origin. Moral education, like culture itself, depends on memory. Education is memory. The need for self-narrative is fulfilled by understanding the narrative of culture that is human history. Without the ability to think in terms of the past, present, and future it is impossible to form a principle of conduct, to see oneself as acting within events and forming judgments of them.

What we find in Cassirer and Vico is a way for the individual to become educated in history. Moral judgments require a knowledge of how to understand historical events. From this understanding of human events writ large, the individual can acquire a base from which to understand the human self as developmental. Only if the self can see itself as a process, and not simply as a substance with inherent properties, can the self have a grasp of freedom as self-determination.

3

Human Nature and Education

Dewey and Cassirer on Human Nature

The question of the nature of human nature is one of the perennial questions of philosophy. Once introduced by Socrates in the beginning of the *Phaedrus* where he wonders whether he is a beast more savage than Typhon or whether he is a simpler animal that has a divine and gentler nature, the question of what a human being is never leaves philosophy as it never leaves the Platonic dialogues. The question of the nature of human nature involves the nature of human education because how human nature is understood determines the sense in which the self can come to know itself—the sense in which the self can develop or educate itself. This education is always, in essence, moral education because it has at its center Socrates' question of whether he is only an animal solely driven by his passions or whether he has the divine power of reason to direct his conduct.

Two of the most widely read philosophical books in contemporary philosophy have been Ernst Cassirer's *An Essay on Man* and John Dewey's *Human Nature and Conduct*. Although Cassirer's *Essay* appeared more than two decades after Dewey's *Human Nature and Conduct*, it is a summary and restatement of the views Cassirer developed in the three volumes of the *Philosophy of Symbolic Forms*, as mentioned earlier. Cassirer quotes a long passage from *Human Nature and Conduct* in his chapter on "The Definition of Man in Terms of Human Culture." He agrees with Dewey's view that it is a mistake to analyze human being into various instincts and reduce human nature to the actions of one or more of them. Like Dewey, Cassirer sees this as a revival in modern terms of scholasticism or "faculty-psychology."

Cassirer also quotes a long passage from *Experience and Nature* regarding the importance of "feeling-qualities" as basic elements of human reality. He says: "The best and clearest statement of this problem has to my mind been given by John Dewey."[1] Cassirer agrees with Dewey that the way in which things are felt, as poignant, beautiful, annoying, harsh, fearful, etc., are traits in experience as fundamental as colors, sounds, smells, tastes, etc. Cassirer regards these feeling-qualities as the content of mythical perception that is at the basis of human culture.

What can be learned by putting together these two very vital accounts of human nature, society, and culture? What might such a union imply for a concept of human education?

An Essay on Man and *Human Nature and Conduct* are two sides of a coin. Cassirer and Dewey are different thinkers but they have more in common in these two works than in disagreement. They both are attempting to work their way forward from the turn of the century developments of Kantian and Hegelian idealism and in so doing to come to grips with the new achievements in biology and the social sciences. Both books in their subtitles purport to be an introduction to a new field of thought: (Cassirer) "An Introduction to a Philosophy of Human Culture" and (Dewey) "An Introduction to Social Psychology"; however, Dewey makes clear in his preface to the first edition that his work does not purport to be a comprehensive treatment of social psychology but only to show that an understanding of habit is the key to such investigation and Cassirer says it is not his intention to impose a ready-made theory on his readers.

Cassirer differs from Dewey in that he never moved from his modification of idealism into a system of cultural forms to a pragmatic viewpoint. Dewey differs from Cassirer in that he did not develop within his standpoint of "pragmatic naturalism" a full theory of the symbol or symbolic form, although he comes close to this especially in *Logic, The Theory of Inquiry*. There are many specific differences but my purpose is to consider the connections of these two works. They have both been so widely read not only by professional philosophers but also by students and persons in other fields because they offer us a way to see the human individual, society, and culture as elements of a whole.

Both Cassirer and Dewey begin their conceptions of human nature from the Aristotelian definitions of the human being as a rational and a social animal. Both Cassirer and Dewey see the human being as a certain kind of animal that differs from other organisms in degree and kind. But the human being is truly part of the biological world and must be approached in these terms. It is not language as such that distinguishes humans from

---

1. Cassirer, *Essay on Man*, 78.

other animals, nor is it sociality or social order. Other animals exhibit linguistic behavior and comprehension, although neither Cassirer nor Dewey could have been aware in their time of the extent to which this has been shown in recent research. Human beings are social animals but social order is not an exclusive feature of human life. Various other organisms relate to each other in social terms and form societies. Distinctive to human beings for Cassirer is what he calls culture, which is based on the uniquely human grasp of symbols.

Dewey employs the word "culture" widely in his writings but in *Human Nature and Conduct* he focuses on the eighteenth-century conception of "morals." Morals in this sense was the study of distinctively human activities. It was the study of those activities in which human beings attempt to explore and confront their own humanity. Dewey refers to Hume as having this purpose in *A Treatise of Human Nature* and other writings in which he was seeking a science of custom. Both Dewey and Cassirer regard human life as distinctively involved in the phenomenon of freedom. Cassirer says at the end of his *Essay*: "Human culture taken as a whole may be described as the process of man's progressive self-liberation."[2] The final part of Dewey's *Human Nature* concerns morality and freedom. Dewey says: "Intelligence is the key to freedom" and "Freedom is the 'truth of necessity' only when we use one 'necessity' to alter another."[3]

Freedom for both Cassirer and Dewey depends upon our ability to alter the conditions of life and to alter the conditions of our own making. Cassirer strongly emphasizes the human power to form the world through the symbol as allowing distance from the immediacy of existence. We can separate ourselves from the world. Dewey insists on our ability to stand apart from existing laws and customs, from the necessity they impose on us, and to envision and act in terms of ideals that support our power of choice. The freedom of the individual to form moral ideals is the essence of moral education. To see ourselves as free requires that we understand the connection of human freedom to our power of self-determination.

Symbol and Habit

The key for a philosophy of culture for Cassirer is *symbol*. The key for a social psychology for Dewey is *habit*. What does Cassirer mean by *symbol*?

2. Ibid., 228.
3. Dewey, *Human Nature*, 304, 312.

What does Dewey mean by *habit*? And, what is the connection between them? As mentioned earlier, Cassirer defines man as a symbolizing animal: "instead of defining man as an *animal rationale*, we should define him as an *animal symbolicum*. By so doing we can designate his specific difference, and we can understand the new way open to man—the way to civilization."[4] In connecting rationality to symbolization Cassirer is seeking to ground reason in the medium or cultural phenomenon that makes human culture possible. Cassirer claims that there is a "crisis in man's knowledge of himself." In past ages the question of "what is man?" has been investigated in terms of an established context such as reason in the ancient world or religion and faith in the Middle Ages. In the modern world the theory of man has lost its intellectual center: "Nietzsche proclaims the will to power, Freud signalizes the sexual instinct, Marx enthrones the economic instinct. Each theory becomes a Procrustean bed on which the empirical facts are stretched to fit a preconceived patter."[5]

There is no one field of inquiry that provides primary access to the human: "Theologians, scientists, politicians, sociologists, biologists, psychologists, ethnologists, economists all approached the problem from their own viewpoints."[6] Cassirer regards each of the areas of human cultural activity as a framework of self-knowledge, a form in which the self realizes an aspect of its own nature. The key for the definition of man that does not reduce the human to some particular instinct or drive and that does not give priority to some one field of inquiry is to define man as the whole of human cultural activity. One form of cultural life is not more "symbolic" than is another; all are orders of experience based on symbols.

These modes of symbolic formation are manifest in the general arena of human cultural activity. The task of the philosopher for Cassirer is to understand the particular logic of each symbolic form and to grasp how they are interconnected to form a whole of culture. This philosophical task includes showing the harmony of all the symbolic forms while preserving the "tonality" of each. Philosophy as a cultural force acts against the tendency for any one form of culture to dominate the others in a given age.

Cassirer explains the presence of the power to form experience through symbols in terms of the biologist Jakob von Uexküll's conception of the organism. On Uexküll's view each organism has its own world: "In

---

4. Cassirer, *Essay on Man*, 26.
5. Ibid., 21.
6. Ibid.

the world of a fly, says Uexküll, we find only 'fly things'; in the world of a sea urchin we find only 'sea urchin things.'"[7] Each organism from the lowest and most simple to the highest and most complex exists in a *functional circle*. Each organism according to its anatomical structure possesses a *receptor system* whereby it responds passively to the world or takes in its experience and an *effector system* whereby it acts toward the world, takes action in relation to the stimuli it receives.

Cassirer says that in the functional system of the human organism we find what can be described as a third system, a *symbol system*. This lets the human being live in a totally new dimension of reality, one in which it constructs a kind of second nature or culture beyond the natural forces to which it responds and which it affects. Once in possession of the power of the symbol to transform immediate experience into meanings, symbols can be used to generate meanings from other symbols. This is as far as Cassirer goes here in grounding his conception of the human being as *animal symbolicum* in the organic world. In so doing he suggests a biological basis for his theory of knowledge and culture but he does not offer a social psychology that would stand between this biology and his cultural epistemology. For this one must turn to Dewey. Cassirer does not have a theory of human conduct to underlie his theory of human culture.

Dewey's Conception of Habit

Dewey and Cassirer both understand human nature in functional, not substantial, terms. This is to say that man is not a particular substance with an essence such that a metaphysical grasp of this would allow us to determine what man is. Instead, for Dewey and Cassirer the nature of human beings can be known by what human beings do. From this perspective human beings acting in terms of and against the forces and necessities of nature that bear down upon them make their own nature through their unique abilities. Human beings realize themselves as human through their own conduct and their culture that depends on it. To have culture in Cassirer's terms requires society. To make human society, as Dewey shows, requires human habit, character, custom, intelligence, and morality.

As Cassirer builds his conception of culture on the symbol, Dewey builds his conception of society on habit. Society is not a rational, contractual association among individuals. The individual is born into society

7. Ibid., 23.

from the beginning. Human life and nature are social from the start. An organism cannot survive without habits. Dewey says: "Habits may be profitably compared to physiological functions, like breathing, digesting."[8] Physiological functions are involuntary but develop as necessary requirements to the social environment. We cannot choose not to have habits. Dewey says: "All habits are demands for certain kinds of activity; and they constitute the self."[9] The self is a system of habits. Dewey says: "Character is the interpretation of habits.... A man can give himself away in a look or a gesture. Character can be real through the medium of individual acts."[10]

Our ability to modify habits is not only crucial to our survival but it is the basis of the moral situation. From habit Dewey can derive custom because customs are habits collectively enacted: "To a considerable extent customs, or widespread uniformities of habit, exist because individuals face the same situation and react in like fashion."[11] Habit does not itself yield intelligence. The functions of mind that are crucial to intelligence require the connection of impulse with habit. Dewey says: "A certain delicate combination of habit and impulse is requisite for observation, memory and judgment."[12] To be intelligent is to develop the ability to allow impulse both to play against habit and to allow habit to form or incorporate what occurs by impulse. The unintelligent mind is simply impulsive or tenacious, holding on only to what it already has.

Dewey describes reason in terms much like Cassirer's notion of a harmony between the symbolic forms of culture. Dewey says: "Rationality, once more, is not a force to evoke against impulse and habit. It is the attainment of a working harmony among diverse desires." These desires in Cassirer's terms would be manifest within various symbolic forms. Dewey continues: "'Reason' as a noun signifies the happy cooperation of a multitude of dispositions, such as sympathy, curiosity, explanation, experimentation, frankness, pursuit—to follow things through—circumspection, to look about at the context, etc., etc."[13] The fact that we as human beings have this power of holding together in a single self this multitude of dispositions

---

8. Dewey, *Human Nature*, 14.
9. Ibid., 25.
10. Ibid., 38.
11. Ibid., 58.
12. Ibid., 117.
13. Ibid., 196.

makes feasible the claim that we can grasp and pursue culture as a whole rather than as a field of fragmented activities.

Dewey's conception of human conduct, based in his analysis of habit, provides us with a picture of the self as grounded in social process that is required for Cassirer's conception of human culture that tends always toward the theory of knowledge without a theory of society to underpin it. The two books go nicely together and provide a basis for thinking through questions of knowledge in relation to questions of psychology and in relation to biology.

Spirit, Life, and Habit

A further question concerns whether symbolic forms are cultural universals in a sense different from habits that are not. Do symbolic forms designate patterns that occur in all cultures? To what extent are Dewey's habits parallel to Cassirer's symbolic forms? If symbolic forms are cultural universals, they would appear to be different in regard to the fact that habits change over time and habits can cease to fulfill their intended consequences although habit itself is a universal of the human world.

In his metaphysics, *Experience and Nature*, Dewey says: "Human learning and habit-forming present thereby an integration of organic-environmental connections so vastly superior to those of animals without language that its experience appears to be super-organic."[14] This is very close to the view of the speech act that Cassirer describes in the *Philosophy of Symbolic Forms: The Metaphysics of Symbolic Forms*. Cassirer says: "The speech act is never in this sense an act of mere assimilation; rather, it is, in however small a way, a creative act, an act of shaping and reshaping."[15]

Although habits can exist in isolation and as such tend to shape behavior in terms of monotonous regularity, Dewey holds that habits also tend to form dynamic systems of behavior. He says: "Communication not only increases the number and variety of habits, but tends to link them subtly together, and eventually to subject habit-forming in a particular case to the habit of recognizing that new modes of association will exact a new use of it. Thus habit is formed in view of possible future changes and does not harden so readily."[16] This conception of habits as interactive regards habits

---

14. Dewey, *Experience and Nature*, 280.
15. Cassirer, *Philosophy of Symbolic Forms*, 4:16.
16. Dewey, *Experience and Nature*, 281.

as flexible and changing according to the conditions that influence behavior. Habit in this sense can be self-modifying. Cassirer in parallel fashion holds that speech acts are not isolated events. He says: "We have here instead an interaction of forces, of impulses of movement. Every use, no matter how transient and temporary, of a linguistic form is such an impulse, which does not leave the world of linguistic forms in the same condition in which it had found it, but which affects it as a whole, which it changes, however imperceptibly, and makes receptive for future new formations."[17] Although Cassirer does not bring this out, speech acts are a kind of behavior that function in terms of habitual patterns. The meanings of such acts are bound up with and in turn direct patterns of human behavior.

Both Dewey and Cassirer have a process-based rather than a substance-based metaphysics of human nature and human being. The *being* of human being is defined by those forms of activity that are distinctive to the human organism. In *Logic, The Theory of Inquiry* Dewey grounds logical thinking in habit. He says: "every inferential conclusion that is drawn involves a habit (either by way of expressing it or initiating it) in the *organic* sense of habit, since life is impossible without ways of action sufficiently general to be properly named *habits*. At the onset, the habit that operates in an inference is purely biological. It operates without our being aware of it."[18] Logical inference, upon which inquiry depends, is based on our ability to connect what is otherwise diverse in experience through habit. Dewey says: "Any habit is a way or manner of action, not a particular act or deed. When it is formulated it becomes, as far as it is accepted, a rule, or more generally, a principle or 'law' of action."[19] Dewey claims there are undeniably habits of inference that may be stated as rules or principles. This would mean, for example, that *modus ponens* is a rule of inference that originally arises from habit.

There is a parallel to Dewey's conception of the basis of inference in the phenomenon of habit in Cassirer's interpretation of the "concept of group." The concept of group is originally a mathematical concept that can be defined "as the totality of unique operations $a, b, c, \ldots$ so that from the combination of any two operations a and b there results an operation c which also belongs to the totality."[20] Put in general terms this means "a

---

17. Cassirer, *Philosophy of Symbolic Forms*, 4:17.
18. Dewey, *Logic*, 12.
19. Ibid., 13.
20. Cassirer, *Symbol, Myth, and Culture*, 274.

group is a set of operations having the property that when two operations are carried out in succession the result is one that would be reached by a simple operation of the set."[21] Cassirer sees in this a principle that runs through the formal structures of human knowledge from mathematics to the physical sciences and that also is the key to the psychology of perception. It is the principle of "perceptual constancy" that shows the inner form of the sameness of the objects we perceive in our surroundings.[22] The factor c accounts for the consistency we experience in the world of objects made from the combination of a and b. This consistency, or to use a Deweyian term, "felt regularity" in experience allows for habit. Habit presupposes this consistency and makes it a principle of action. *Modus ponens* can only function if its terms remain constant. Habit in turn influences perception. They are aspects of a totality of process.

Cassirer's main metaphysical distinction, as mentioned earlier, is between life (*Leben*) and spirit (*Geist*). Cassirer takes this distinction from the idealist tradition, most specifically from his reading of Hegel. A version of it is to be found in Dewey which is not surprising given Dewey's familiarity with Hegelian philosophy. Cassirer says: "the opposition between 'Leben' and 'Geist' is the hub of this metaphysics."[23] Life as a metaphysical principle is a continual flux without pause but it is not simply universal force. It has a duality within itself; its tendency to universality is offset by a tendency toward concrete particularity. Immanent in life is its self-transcendence as form. The opposition between life and spirit is functional, that is, when life generates itself as spirit, its movement becomes that of the self-developing forms of spirit. Life and spirit are two aspects of the general organic process that underlies the symbolic forms of human culture.

Dewey says, "As life is a character of events in a peculiar condition of organization, and 'feeling' is a quality of life-forms marked by complexly mobile and discriminating responses, so 'mind' is an added property assumed by a feeling creature, when it reaches that organized interaction with other living creatures which is language communication."[24] What Dewey designates as "mind" is what Cassirer means by "*Geist*" ("mind" being in fact another way to translate *Geist* into English). Of mind Dewey says: "But the whole history of science, art, and morals proves that the mind that

---

21. Ibid., 274–75.
22. Ibid., 286–87.
23. Cassirer, *Philosophy of Symbolic Forms*, 4:8.
24. Dewey, *Experience and Nature*, 258.

appears *in* individuals is not as such individual mind."[25] Mind for Dewey is as *Geist* is for Cassirer, writ large in culture. Dewey builds his metaphysical account of mind on the biology and psychology of the organism. Cassirer's metaphysics is driven most directly by his epistemology.

As discussed in Chapter 1, Cassirer gives a phenomenological grounding for his metaphysics in his essay on "Basis Phenomena." To recall them here: Cassirer describes these phenomena in various ways but in general they are I, act, and the work. The "I" is the locus of life in the human self, the "monad." "Act" is the phenomenon of will or action in relation to an other. It is the basis of ethical experience. The "work" (*das Werk*) is a lasting cultural product, something made by the I in its action that becomes a part of culture. Cassirer says, "every work is as such not that of an individual, but proceeds from cooperative correlative action. It bears witness to 'social' action."[26] Culture is itself a work that is made up of works, the ultimate forms of which are symbolic forms such as myth, religion, language, art, history, law, technology, politics, and science. For Cassirer the basis phenomena are not derived from anything. They are the fundamental elements of human existence. When the I interacts with the other to produce a work, human culture is the result in all of its basic forms.

Cassirer's symbolic forms are universals of human culture. Wherever one finds a particular human culture these forms are present, although their particular modalities vary from one culture to another. Thus the art of one culture will vary from the art of another; their languages will differ; they will each have different histories, laws, systems of politics, etc. But every culture will have language, art, etc. This is true also of science. A given culture may not have science developed in a theoretical-mathematical form such as is familiar to us, but every culture will have forms of empirical-practical knowledge. New symbolic forms do not arise. All of them are always present in any actual culture in an explicit, articulate manner or in a proto-manner. Any given culture may develop one form over others even to the detriment of the others. Thus there can be a strongly scientific and technological culture or a strongly aesthetically oriented culture or a culture that is predominately legalistic and historical. The dominance or balance of these symbolic forms can shift at different periods of a particular culture's life.

---

25. Ibid., 219.
26. Cassirer. *Philosophy of Symbolic Forms*, 4:159.

Dewey's conception of habit as connected to patterns of learning and language is a human universal. All human beings create patterns of conduct through habit, as do animals. But unlike animals, human habit formation is connected to culture. Dewey says: "Language in its widest sense—that is, including all means of communication such as, for example, monuments, rituals, and formalized arts—is the medium in which culture exists and through which it is transmitted."[27] Where Dewey uses the term "language," Cassirer uses the wider term "symbol," language being for Cassirer one form of symbol-use. Since the period in which Dewey and Cassirer were forming their views, it has become increasingly evident that there are examples of patterns of language-use, communication, tool-use, and societal behavior in the animal world that are not as different in kind from those of the human world as Dewey and Cassirer believed. But their general point still holds that only human beings create a total world of culture that involves the productions of works of art, histories, science, etc. The key to human culture and the patterns of human life for both Dewey and Cassirer is that human activity and human life are self-modifying. For Dewey this means that habits are themselves flexible and can also be modified by judgment. For Cassirer this means that the power to symbolize includes the power to develop systems of symbols that create their own worlds of meaning.

Implications for Human Education

What might be the implications of this way of thinking for human education? Dewey's philosophy of education is a topic in its own right. It has not only been the most written about aspect of his philosophy, it has been the most influential. In fact, Dewey's ideas on education have had more impact on modern American society than the ideas on any subject by any other modern philosopher. Philosophy has rarely been such a force in its time. My aim here is not to examine or re-examine Dewey's philosophy of education, but only to suggest a perspective on education that emerges from the combination of Cassirer's conception of culture and Dewey's social psychology of conduct.

Dewey says: "Education becomes the art of taking advantage of the helplessness of the young; the forming of habits becomes a guarantee for the maintenance of hedges of custom."[28] Cassirer points to Aristotle's view

---

27. Dewey, *Logic*, 20.
28. Dewey, *Human Nature*, 64.

that "all human knowledge originates from a basic tendency of human nature manifesting itself in man's most elementary actions and reactions. The whole extent of the life of the senses is determined by and impregnated with this tendency."[29] This combined Cassirerian-Deweyian view is against specialization in human education. Specialization is not bad in itself. It is the basis of professional training but it needs to be grounded in an earlier experience of general education.

Cassirer's range of symbolic forms from myth to science implies a theory of general education. Since each of these symbolic forms of cultural life is a form of self-knowledge, the individual human being must enter into all of them in order to explore fully the dimensions of the self. We can only overcome the fragmentation of knowledge and culture that we find in the modern world by promoting an education of the whole. A curriculum at almost any level of education could be organized around Cassirer's list of symbolic forms. The way in which the student would be taught myth or science or history, for example, would vary according to the student's age and intellectual development as is done now. The important point would be to keep the student in touch with all these forms, not to allow one to dominate education any more than a given form should dominate culture itself.

There is not only a principle of general education implicit in Cassirer's view; there is also a principle of diversity. It offers a functional approach to the current interest in cultural diversity, but an approach not fully realized. Education of the student in the nature of human culture itself would uniquely equip the student to study and grasp individual cultures. Without a grasp of the basic structure of human culture itself, the student has no knowledge of what to look for in studying a particular culture and thus may just fix on anything with no way to grasp it as a whole and as a part of human culture as a whole.

If we add to these views of a cultural approach to education Dewey's conceptions of habit and intelligence, something more emerges. The student is not simply to be given information. Dewey's comment about education being the taking advantage of the young is a criticism of basing education in habits of rote learning and acceptance of the authority of custom. In our day the fascination with information and the acquiring of information plays the role of what Dewey is criticizing in his day. Finding information and manipulating it is not thinking. Intelligence, which involves observation, memory, and judgment, requires the combination of

---

29. Cassirer, *Essay on Man*, 2.

habit and impulse as Dewey claims. To think requires the student to be able to move from one context to another. In Cassirer's terms, this is to move from one symbolic form to another and from one culture to another. Cassirer's formulation of Aristotle's desire to know points to the fact that there is always an impulse to go beyond what is settled in habit and custom, to go beyond information. Information is not bad in itself. It is a necessary part of education but it is not all of education.

Education must remain open to this natural activity of the impulse to know. Habit is the stability of mind that tempers impulse. What seems established in habit and custom in the student's own culture is challenged by an encounter with the habits and customs of another culture. This opposition of actual patterns of mind and life is what stimulates observation, memory, and judgment. The attempt by the student to confront this opposition as active forces, not merely as additional information about something, introduces the experience of moral deliberation. The world cannot be reduced to a simple viewpoint and the nature of the opposition and its relation to the whole of human culture and life must be thought through. This involves proceeding from the settled state of affairs to the formulation of ideals. Once an ideal is in mind, the student begins to gain experience in the power of moral judgment. The self encounters itself as a force through which it makes its world, as the maker of knowledge and culture.

Dewey's conception of intelligence coupled with Cassirer's sense of culture becomes the basis for the process of moral education or the education of the self into its own nature and limits. With today's strong involvement in information, technology, and specialization, the education of the human self into its own nature is easily forgotten or at least slighted. Cassirer and Dewey offer us reminders of this other dimension to education and their combined conception of the human offers us a powerful perspective on how to accomplish it.

Conclusion

The human world for both Dewey and Cassirer is a world of moral or ethical freedom because it is a world of self-determination. There is a positive and negative side to both habit and symbolic form. The positive side is typified by the above-mentioned positive powers of each. The negative side of habit is that we can become entrenched in rote ways of accomplishing things. Judgment must play a role in modifying these ways in relation to changing conditions. The negative side of symbolic forms is that one form of symbolism may come to dominate over the others. This can occur for Cassirer in times of social crisis such as when mythic images take over political processes to the detriment of reason and social analysis.

Cassirer's and Dewey's metaphysics of human experience differ in "tonality" but they share a common vision that is significant for human education. I expressed views on the implications of their positions for education earlier in this chapter. But several more remarks can be made that follow from Dewey's and Cassirer's metaphysics. What I am calling their common vision is that human culture is at base the manifestation of human freedom. Human culture for Dewey and Cassirer is not alienation, although individuals can become alienated from culture and understandably so when systems of injustice prevail. But culture in itself is not a process of alienation. Rightly understood it is a process of self-determination, a process wherein the human self can realize its own nature in all of its aspects. In times of social crisis and injustice it is this sense of self-determination that must be asserted and reaffirmed. The power of self-determination is at the basis of human being, that out of which all human cultures originally arise.

How can this sense of freedom as self-determination be taught? There does not appear to be a method or simple formula to accomplish such a sense of things. Teaching and education must be done in terms of an ideal, otherwise learning is simply rote learning of a subject matter. If the teacher has this ideal actively in mind, it will come out in various ways to the student. An ideal is a force in the mind that will always effect an orientation and make itself known. An ideal to be anything must first be understood in its own terms and these include how it is part of human reality. To understand what Dewey and Cassirer have said is crucial to grasping their common ideal of human freedom. Any teacher could use their work as a basis of individual study to grasp more fully this ideal. But if one were to proceed more pragmatically, one could imagine programs, workshops, seminars, and discussions in which this ideal could be considered in the concrete, that is, in relation to particular courses and subject matters. There is no general formula. A powerful ideal can only take root in the particular situation and become part of the rapport and communication between student and teacher. In the end this ideal has to enter the distinctively human relationship that is at the basis of the educational process.

4

Pragmatism and Idealism

The Pragmatic-Pluralist Tradition

Two principles fundamental to classic American pragmatism as represented by William James and John Dewey are pluralism of thought and the education of the individual. These principles are regarded by pragmatic philosophy as keys to the maintenance of democratic society. They parallel the two principles upon which the nineteenth-century German university was based, namely *Lehrfreiheit* (freedom to teach) and *Lernfreiheit* (freedom to learn). Human knowledge requires the freedom to be considered and pursued in any manner a thinker may formulate. Human education requires the freedom to entertain ideas without any doctrinal restrictions. Pragmatism, then, supports what we may call the morality of freedom. Underlying this position is the idealist conception of human freedom as not simply freedom from restrictions, but the power of the individual to be self-developing toward an ideal of the moral or the Good. This freedom is the Socratic license to pursue such an ideal toward whatever end reason takes us.

Although the pluralist tradition in American thought has close connections with the philosophies of William James and John Dewey and with pragmatism generally, but philosophies in the idealist tradition have not been commonly associated with pluralism. The idealist insistence on system has stood in contrast to the open-ended sense of pragmatic inquiry. Both critical idealism and absolute idealism, each in its own way, tend toward monism. Critical idealism is based on the singleness of the transcendental method to establish the basis of philosophical knowledge. Hegelian idealism with its teleology of the Absolute was accused by James of the monism of a "block universe." Cassirer's philosophy of symbolic forms as discussed earlier combines elements from both Kantian and Hegelian idealism, but in its fully developed form as a philosophy of human culture, I wish to argue, it takes on a pluralist character. It is perhaps the one form of twentieth-century idealism that truly embodies a pluralist ideal, more so, for example, than does the idealism of Benedetto Croce or R. G. Collingwood.

The birth of pluralism in the United States can be traced back to the conversations that took place in the philosophical club meetings in Boston in the 1870s of which Borden Parker Bowne and George Holmes Howison were prominent members and who later were led to the personalist movement. Jean Wahl in his *Pluralist Philosophies of England and America* credits Bowne as the first to use "pluralism" in English, Wahl attributes the original use of the term to Rudolf Hermann Lotze's *Metaphysik* (1879). The spirit of Lotze's philosophy is pluralistic in that he held that all philosophical systems should remain open to new possibilities rather than claim completeness and thus close off inquiry.

To my knowledge Cassirer's philosophy has not been interpreted in any detail as a form of pluralism. I wish to consider two questions: (1) in what sense can Cassirer's philosophy of symbolic forms be rightly described as pluralistic; and (2) to what extent does Cassirer's philosophy contribute to the possibilities of pluralism as an ideal of philosophical inquiry and of moral philosophy?

Two Senses of "Pluralism"

Cassirer does not employ the term "*Pluralismus*." He would have encountered it, however, in Lotze and he would have encountered its spirit of openness through Lotze's role in relation to the various schools of neo-Kantianism at the turn of the twentieth century. Hajo Holborn, the historian and Cassirer's colleague at Yale, said at the memorial service for Cassirer in 1945, "Ernst Cassirer began his studies when the new philosophical movement had already gained influence in German universities. Lotze was probably the chief bridge-builder between the classic idealism and the neo-idealism which then found its leaders in Dilthey and the neo-Kantian schools of Marburg and the South-West, represented by Cohen and Natorp [Cassirer's teachers] and by Windelband and Rickert."[1]

Lotze is the source for Cassirer's theory of "qualifying concepts" that is the basis of his theory of class-concepts in his examination of language as a symbolic form in the first volume of the *Philosophy of Symbolic Forms*.

---

1. Schilpp, ed., *Philosophy of Ernst Cassirer*, 42.

Lotze shows how the class-concepts of logic require the primordial power of language to form qualities directly as concepts that later came to be those features that define classes. By apprehending each of the qualities of any given object as themselves separate and concrete entities rather than as aspects that inhere in a constant object, language, according to Lotze, expresses a "first universal."[2] This sense of a first universal leads directly to Cassirer's conception of myth as a first form of "thinking." "Mythical thought" is the subject of the second volume of the *Philosophy of Symbolic Forms*. Myth is the product of what Cassirer in the third volume of this work calls the "expressive function" (*Ausdrucksfunktion*) of consciousness. This function is the first stage of Cassirer's phenomenology of knowledge that is the basis of Cassirer's whole philosophy of cultural activity.

Cassirer's own approach to philosophy from his earliest works forward was always one of "bridge-building" between past and present philosophies, among various types of philosophical inquiry, and among various fields of knowledge. Cassirer made constant use of the history of philosophy. He states, as quoted previously in my Preface: "the custom, which has once more become popular, of hurling one's ideas into empty space as it were, without inquiring into their relation to the general development of scientific philosophy, has never struck me as fruitful."[3] Cassirer saw his position as always open to development. In response to Martin Heidegger's attempt at their famous debate at Davos, Switzerland (1929) to confine his philosophy to Marburg neo-Kantianism, Cassirer firmly replied that neo-Kantianism must be understood in "functional terms"; that is, as capable of developing itself as a series of positions in response to other points of view.[4] Cassirer modified Marburg neo-Kantianism, departing from it progressively beginning with his first work of systematic philosophy, *Substance and Function* (1910). Cassirer eventually includes aspects of Hegel's philosophy and draws on thinkers in the general tradition of *Lebensphilosophie* such as Max Scheler with whose anthropology he does not fully agree, and with Georg Simmel's conception of culture and alienation with whom he also does not agree.[5] Cassirer's spirit of philosophizing was more one of synthesizing in order to move ideas forward than that of refutation and exclusive

---

2. Cassirer, *Philosophy of Symbolic Forms*, 1:282.
3. Ibid., 3:xvi.
4. Hamburg, "Seminar," 213–22.
5. Cassirer, *Cultural Studies*, 103–27.

command of the truth. In this sense his approach to philosophy embodies a pluralist ideal.

As an English word in general use "pluralism" has two principal senses: one is distinctively philosophical; the other is political or social. These same two senses also are attached to the German cognate, *Pluralismus*. In the first sense "pluralism" characterizes a metaphysical position holding that reality is composed of a plurality of independent entities. It is contrasted with monism and usually also with dualism, even though dualism is technically plural. As a metaphysical term "pluralism" holds that there are varying kinds of ultimate reality. In the second sense "pluralism" refers to a state of society in which diverse racial, ethnic, religious, or social groups maintain their individual identities and traditions within the limits of a single society or nation. "Pluralism" in this second sense can refer not only to this actual state of affairs; it can also designate a theory that advocates this form of society.

We may add an epistemological corollary to the first or metaphysical sense of pluralism, namely that there are multiple ways of knowing the world. There is no exclusive or single way of knowing that produces truth thus making all other methods or forms of mind ways of error. An epistemological monism closes off in advance alternative ways of knowing the world and occupies itself with shoring up the exclusivity of its position.

We may add to the sense of pluralism as a concept of social diversity an ideal specific to philosophy as a human institution. Applied to philosophy as a distinctively human endeavor, pluralism implies that within the philosophical community of scholars each philosophical position has a right to representation, a right to be heard and not dismissed by a dominant opposing position as "not philosophy." Pluralism in this respect is a concept of philosophical toleration, not simply an endorsement of philosophical eclecticism.

Any philosophy can be considered as made of partial truths that as such open up further possibilities. This sense of pluralism need not entail philosophical historicism, although it could. A given philosophy, on this view, may succeed another by taking the presuppositions of the earlier position as propositions to be questioned, the response to which forms the basis of the new position. But in so doing, it is not necessary to reduce the search for truth to the conditions of the search. A pluralist approach can allow for truth as a transhistorical ideal. Cassirer gives a formulation of this ideal: "'Truth' is not bound to productive activity and is not to be measured by its criteria."[6] As an ideal of philosophical community pluralism allows for the consideration of both historicist and non-historicist conceptions of truth. My point is only that pluralism does not commit its advocate to the view that truth is wholly relative to the conditions of its production.

How does Cassirer's philosophy of symbolic forms fit into the two senses of pluralism described above? Is Cassirer's idealism an epistemological monism in the sense of limiting knowledge to acts of scientific cognition in which logical categories are employed to determine the nature of the object? Is Cassirer's idealism a type of metaphysical monism in the Hegelian sense?[7] Cassirer's philosophy of symbolic forms at its base contains elements of both Kant's transcendental method and Hegel's dialectic.

A Further Look at the Philosophy of Symbolic Forms

Cassirer expands Kant's transcendental understanding from science, morality, and aesthetic and organic forms of experience to myth, religion, language, art, history, and science. He says in this expansion "the critique of reason becomes the critique of culture."[8] Cassirer, as pointed out earlier, also mentions but does not discuss the possibility of various forms of social life such as economics, technology, customary ethics (*Sitte*), and law.[9] Cassirer does away with the Kantian thing-in-itself and with the distinction between the constitutive application of the categories to the phenomenal object and the regulative ideas. For Cassirer there are not two senses of the object of knowledge, one that is accessible to the knower and one that is in principle beyond the knower's powers properly to apprehend it within experience. There is not a phenomenal given and a noumenal reality beyond it. Through his principle of "symbolic pregnance" Cassirer claims that the given is at once phenomenal and noumenal. All that is known is "cultural," that is, an immediate bond of the sensible and the "spiritual" (*geistig*). For Cassirer we never step outside the human world of culture. All the objects within the circle of human cultural activity are constructed within

---

6. Cassirer, *Philosophy of Symbolic Forms*, 4:187.
7. Ibid., 4:193.
8. Ibid., 1:80.
9. Ibid., 2:xv.

the various forms of culture, not all of which are cognitive or conceptual. "Concepts," Cassirer says, "are not the only approach to reality."[10]

Objectivity, for Cassirer, is not dependent on faith in the existence of the material thing outside us because the "material thing" is itself a construction through our linguistic powers of class formation. Objectivity is defined within each symbolic form of culture in which the subjective and the objective are poles, the nature of which is determined within the specific modality of each form. The full account of objectivity depends upon the power of philosophical thought to show the interconnections among symbolic forms that together are human culture. Cassirer says: "we cannot regard the world of empirical objects as an immediate datum—as a hard and brute fact. Objectivity is, from the point of view of a philosophical analysis, not the *terminus a quo* but the *terminus ad quem*; it is not the starting point but the terminating point of human knowledge."[11]

The key to the transcendental method for Cassirer is the schematism of the first *Critique* in which the concept and the intuition are joined. Kant says the schematism is "an art concealed in the depths of the human soul."[12] Cassirer believes he has uncovered this art in the phenomenon of the symbol. There is for Cassirer no literal interpretation of the world. Any "literal" interpretation of the object is accomplished by symbols. The symbol is a concrete universal. The internal bond between the particularity of the symbol and its universal significance is functional not substantial. This bond is abstractly embodied in what Cassirer designates as the functional concept (*Funktionsbegriff*) or $\phi(x)$. The principle of order in a series of variables represented by ϕ is meaningless in itself. It has significance only in terms of the variables it specifically orders. The series of variables represented by x is a meaningless collection of particulars if considered apart from their order as expressed in their bond with ϕ. Each of the two elements is without significance when taken alone, but together they are a concrete universal.[13]

As discussed in Chapter 2, underlying the functional concept at the level of perception in what may be called Cassirer's life-world is the phenomenon of "symbolic pregnance" (*symbolische Prägnanz*), a term Cassirer takes from the "law of pregnance" of Gestalt psychology. Symbolic pregnance refers to the claim that every particular perception is an act of

---

10. Cassirer, *Symbol, Myth, and Culture*, 183.
11. Ibid., 166.
12. Kant, *Critique of Pure Reason*, 183.
13. Cassirer, *Philosophy of Symbolic Forms*, 3:300.

grasping sense in sensibility (*Sinn im Sinnlichkeit*): the spiritual (*geistig*) is simply there in the sensory. The mind does not engage in an act of perception that is then connected to a meaning. Cassirer claims that Husserl in his descriptive phenomenology did not fully overcome this Kantian disjunction but instead preserves it in a new form in his doctrine of the difference between "hyletic" and "noetic" strata.[14] Cassirer says: "By symbolic pregnance we mean the way in which perception as a sensory experience contains at the same time a certain nonintuitive meaning which it immediately and concretely represents."[15] All symbols have within them the inner dynamic of the tension of the two poles present in symbolic pregnance.

Parallel to this immediate bond between the sensory and the nonintuitive is the bond between the physical presence and the spiritual presence of the symbol. A word is just a breath of air, but at the same time it is the presentation of a meaning. This meaning has a specific place within the totality of meanings that comprise human culture. A mark on paper is just a mound of ink, but at the same time it can be a written word. Even if its meaning cannot be grasped, it is not meaningless because at the least it is a mark with properties of light and dark, having potentially aesthetic qualities.

In his phenomenology of knowledge of the third volume of the *Philosophy of Symbolic Forms* Cassirer offers a thought experiment that stands as his proof for his conception of the symbol. As discussed in Chapter 2, he asks the reader to consider a graph-like drawing, a *Linienzug*. He says the line may be grasped in purely expressive terms giving attention to its shape, to the feeling of movement it conveys, and so forth. We may, however, also respond to it in mathematical terms regarding it as the representation of certain geometric proportions or as representing statistical tendencies. From these ways of apprehending it we may pass to seeing it as a mythical-magical sign delimiting a sacred from a profane sphere. We can further apprehend it as an aesthetic ornament attending to its visual properties having their own intrinsic significance.[16] This plurality of meanings is imminent in even the simplest physical mark.

Cassirer gives a second version of this thought-experiment, as mentioned earlier. He says we may act as though we are Robinson Crusoe abandoned on a desert island with no traces of human culture. Then by chance

---

14. Ibid., 3:197–98.
15. Ibid., 3:202.
16. Ibid., 3;200–201.

we find an unusual stone that attracts our attention. We may first become interested in its physical and chemical properties, its weight and composition. We may go on to consider it from the point of view of a mineralogist or geologist. But on further inspection we realize that the stone has marks on its surface that recur in regular order. These marks begin to appear to us as written characters. With this possibility we are in a human world; we pass from the physical thing into the human world of symbols. The characters, Cassirer says "begin to 'speak' to me. In my perfect seclusion from all human beings I suddenly hear the message of a human world."[17]

Each of the symbolic forms—myth, religion, language, art, history, science—has, Cassirer says, an inner form (*innere Form*). Each offers us a way of intuiting space, time, and number. Each embodies a way of making causal connections and of delimiting objects. Each contains a sense of the subjective or the self. Although each symbolic form contains forms of intuition, categories of thought, and conceptions of the I, each form differs from the others in the way they come together. Each is a complete world that competes with the others for its own form of knowledge and validity.

Philosophy, Cassirer says, is not a symbolic form. It commands no particular use of the symbolic act. Philosophy enters into each of the symbolic worlds of the forms of knowledge and culture and attempts to grasp the unique claims of each in order to comprehend the place of each in the total complex of culture. Cassirer says: "It is characteristic of philosophical knowledge as the 'self-knowledge of reason' that it does not create a principally new symbol form, it does not found in this sense a new creative modality—but it grasps the earlier modalities as that which they are: as characteristic symbolic forms."[18]

Philosophy is the ø in the (x) series of symbolic forms and as such it is the search for their harmony. Cassirer's metaphor for this in *An Essay on Man* is taken from Heraclitus' fragment: "Men do not understand how that which is torn in different directions comes into accord with itself—harmony in contrariety, as in the case of the bow and the lyre."[19] Cassirer sees the duty of philosophy to show that beyond the contrariety that exists naturally among the symbolic forms, "All these functions complete and complement one another. Each one opens a new horizon and shows us a

---

17. Cassirer, *Symbol, Myth, and Culture*, 136.
18. Cassirer, *Philosophy of Symbolic Forms*, 4:226.
19. Cassirer, *Essay on Man*, 222–23.

new aspect of humanity."[20] This conception of philosophy can be grasped as a type of pluralism.

Cassirer and Hegel

Cassirer takes both Kant's transcendental method and the principles of the schematism into all areas of human experience. He joins these to a version of Hegel's claim that "the True is the whole" and applies it to human culture as a whole within which there is a dialectic of symbolic forms. At the beginning of the second volume of the *Philosophy of Symbolic Forms* that contains his theory of mythical thought, Cassirer conceives his task in terms of Hegel's ladder metaphor in the *Phenomenology of Spirit*. He holds that Hegel begins his "science of the experience of consciousness" too high in experience at the level of the thing or object, the level of representation, the *Darstellungsfunktion* of consciousness. Cassirer says he wishes to take the reader a lower and show how all human experience develops from myth.[21] In the third volume of the *Philosophy of Symbolic Forms* Cassirer also begins with Hegel saying that the phenomenology of knowledge he will present does not take "phenomenology" in its modern (Husserlian) sense but in its Hegelian sense.[22] He then proceeds to develop his account of human knowledge from the expressive, to the representational, to the significative function of consciousness.

The general movement of consciousness through these stages is dialectical, one stage giving way through its internal movement to another, but there is no strict principle of *Aufhebung* as found in Hegel's *Phenomenology*. In his dialectic of mythical thought at the end of Volume 2, Cassirer explicitly denies that the dialectic in which myth develops beyond itself toward religion follows a principle of seamless development.[23] Cassirer claims that in culture as a whole, stances of consciousness often sharply confront each other and pass into other positions without one stage being cancelled and preserved, or taken up into the other. Cassirer also claims that Hegel's system ends all of human knowledge in the form of logic and thus is engaged in a reduction of all forms to one, something that Cassirer is at all points

---

20. Ibid., 228.
21. Cassirer, *Philosophy of Symbolic Forms*, 2:xv–xiv.
22. Ibid., 3:xiv.
23. Ibid., 2:235.

in his philosophy determined to reject.[24] Cassirer may be overemphasizing this point to make his point, but whether Cassirer is taking an overly narrow view of Hegel's system is not the issue here.

Cassirer, in fact, does not embrace the classic notion of German philosophy: the system. Instead, as discussed in Chapter 1, he speaks of the need for "systematic review" (*systematischer Rückblick*), systematic reconstruction (*systematische 'Rekonstruktion'*), or "systematic overview" (*systematischer Überblick*).[25] In accord with this approach Cassirer can enter into any content of culture using both Hegel's sense of the whole and Kant's sense of the transcendental and, taking the symbol as medium, he can begin to elicit the meaning of the particular in relation to the totality of the symbolic forms. Any content of culture can be comprehended genetically beginning from its mythical origins and developing to its acme as religion, language, art, history, science and so forth. Cassirer's sense of the systematic as opposed to the drive to system promises philosophical illumination without subscribing to the Hegelian doctrine of the Absolute. At no point in his corpus does Cassirer offer a concept of the Absolute as the unifying philosophical principle. Cassirer says, "The 'Absolute' is always simply the completely relative, which has been carried through to the end in a systematic overview, and the absoluteness of *Geist* in particular can be nothing else and cannot try to be."[26] Systematic review or overview remains open to further interpretation.

If we turn from Cassirer's epistemology of symbolic forms to what he calls the "metaphysics of symbolic forms" we find a further example of his adoption of Hegelian dialectic and the Hegelian conception of *Geist*.[27] In the most general terms what Hegel means by *Geist* Cassirer means by culture. Culture like *Geist* is a whole, but unlike Hegel's *Geist* the symbolic forms and their various developments and oppositions are not resolved into an overriding order. Culture is a totality, but the plurality of forms within it does not exhibit an overarching teleology. Consciousness for Cassirer develops itself through the symbolic forms in a purposive manner but does not do so in terms of a single absolute end. The interrelations among the symbolic forms are functional, meaning that if at any point we consider a specific content of culture, a determinate account of its connections to

24. Ibid., 1:83.
25. Ibid., 4:54–56, 167, 227.
26. Ibid., 4:227.
27. Ibid., 4:3–33.

the other aspects of culture can be given in terms of "systematic review" without the need for an Absolute. At the basis of such a functional account is the fact that the bond of the ø(x) can systematically expand on itself. The ø can itself be a variable so to speak in a superscript series and the (x) so to speak can be an ordering principle in a subscript series. Any functional bond can expand self-reflectively and be determinate at any point without invoking an overriding teleology.

This functional manner of cultural explanation is possible because it is based upon and reflects the very logic of *Geist* itself in its self-development. Cassirer says that only *Geist* "can make distinctions, choose, and judge. This 'judging' of course is—and herein lies perhaps its true depth and its final mystery—such that it is within itself capable of turning around, that as the directive principle it does not make an exception of itself, but rather that it is able to turn against itself."[28] The opposite of *Geist* in Cassirer's metaphysical conception of the symbolic forms is life (*Leben*). Life is an unbroken unity that Cassirer says "rests 'blissfully in itself.'" Life is in no sense self-modifying and its ongoing movement or flow stands in a dialectical opposition to *Geist*. Life and *Geist* are not two substances, standing to each other as two opposing things. Their relationship is functional such that each is actively part of the other's movement of existence. *Geist* is the ø that constantly absorbs and modifies the movement of life, as life produces the variables of x.

The internal movement of *Geist* is accomplished by its constant recapitulation of itself against the forces of life. Cassirer says: "This turnabout, this 'reflection,' entails no break within *Geist* itself; rather, it is the form in which it proves itself and reconfirms itself, something that is characteristic of and typical of it alone."[29] At the basis of the process that is *Geist* is an act of "self-knowledge." What Cassirer puts in metaphysical terms in the fourth volume of the *Philosophy of Symbolic Forms*, he affirms as a principle of the philosophy of culture in the first sentence of *An Essay on Man* "That self-knowledge is the highest aim of philosophical inquiry appears to be generally acknowledged."[30] Philosophy attaches itself to no specific symbolic form. In order to be itself philosophy necessarily attaches itself to and reflects the essence of *Geist* its ability to turnabout in itself. "Life

---

28. Ibid., 4:33.
29. Ibid.
30. Cassirer, *Essay on Man*, 1.

as such," Cassirer says, "knows no such turning back upon itself, no such reaffirmation."[31]

In a fragment concerning "the basic opposition of modern philosophy" Cassirer says "The meaning of 'life' in this sense was more deeply recognized by Fichte, Schelling, and Hegel than by the 'moderns.'"[32] Cassirer regards Hegel's claim in the *Phenomenology of Spirit* that "Substance becomes Subject" as a crucial turning point in the conception of *Geist* as self-developing movement that distinguishes its form of life from that of life as such. Hegel says: "everything turns on grasping and expressing the True, not only as *Substance*, but equally as *Subject*."[33] Cassirer says: "*Geist* attains to the form of life by breaking away from its mere immediacy—this is most obvious in the 'symbolic forms,' in language, art, knowing."[34] *Geist* is Subject in the sense that it has an internal life, an inner form that is variously manifested in the inner form of each of the symbolic forms.

Although Cassirer moves very skillfully beyond Marburg neo-Kantianism and from Kant toward Hegel employing many figures such as Leibniz, Wilhelm von Humboldt, Schelling, Vico, and Goethe, he is clear that he does not see Kantianism as simply turning into Hegelianism. He says, "I do not think that we can construct a continuous process of thought by which we are led from the premises of Kant's Critique to the principles and results of the metaphysics of Hegel. Instead, on the harmony between Hegel and Kant we must, to my mind, lay stress upon the fundamental, the intrinsic and ineradicable opposition between the two systems."[35] This insistence on the fact that the Hegelian philosophy is not the natural continuance of the Kantian shows how strongly Cassirer is committed to the preservation of a dialectic of oppositions without their necessary resolution in a teleology of *Aufhebungen*. Cassirer is strongly pluralistic in this respect. He genuinely takes from both Kant and Hegel but he does not consider his own position to synthesize or resolve the real differences between the two.

---

31. Cassirer, *Philosophy of Symbolic Forms*, 4:33.
32. Ibid., 4:227–28.
33. Hegel, *Phenomenology*, 17.
34. Cassirer, *Philosophy of Symbolic Forms*, 4:228.
35. Cassirer, *Symbol, Myth, and Culture*, 109.

Cassirer and the Spirit of Pragmatic Pluralism

The second question originally raised concerns the sense in which Cassirer's philosophy of symbolic forms contains a normative sense of pluralism to guide philosophical inquiry. Something of this ideal has already been suggested in showing how Cassirer reached the major tenets of his position.

In putting forth a definition of man in his *An Essay on Man* Cassirer criticizes the view that intelligence or intelligent behavior is not a distinctive phenomenon of human life but is essentially a type of higher or more developed version of instinct as found throughout animal life. He says, "When used in this way [conceiving intelligence as a kind of instinct] the concept of instinct becomes an example of that typical methodological error which was described by William James as the psychologist's fallacy. The word 'instinct,' which may be useful for the description of animal or human behavior, is hypostatized into a sort of natural power."[36] In relation to this mistaken conception of intelligence as a kind of instinct, Cassirer cites Dewey's criticism in *Human Nature and Conduct* in which Dewey says: "It is unscientific to try to restrict original activities to a definite number of sharply demarcated classes of instincts. And the practical result of this attempt is injurious."[37]

Cassirer considers whether there is an alternative to conceiving human intelligence as simply a means or "instinct" or "bundle of instincts" by which human beings adapt themselves to the conditions of existence. Cassirer says he has attempted to advance such an alternative in the *Philosophy of Symbolic Forms*. He says the method of this work "is not designed to abrogate but to complement former views. The philosophy of symbolic forms starts from the presupposition that, if there is any definition of the nature or 'essence' of man, this definition can only be understood as a functional, not a substantial one." He continues, "Man's outstanding characteristic, his distinguishing mark is not his metaphysical or physical nature—but his work. It is this work, it is the system of human activities, which defines and determines the circle of 'humanity.'"[38] This circle of humanity is in culture as it is in each human individual. It is based on the fact that we confront our own nature in the phenomenon of "work."

36. Cassirer, *Essay on Man*, 66.
37. Dewey, *Human Nature*, 181.
38. Cassirer, *Essay on Man*, 67–68.

Pragmatism and Idealism

As discussed in Chapter 1, Cassirer has in mind here the German word *das Werk* which is what he uses in the fourth volume of the *Philosophy of Symbolic Forms* where he says the *Werk* is one of three basis phenomena that make possible the human world itself, the others being the I and action (*das Wirkens-Phänomen*).[39] The work is not labor (*Arbeit*) but work in the sense of a cultural work (for example an art work), something that is made or an achievement. The work is the key to self-knowledge. Cassirer says, "know your *work* and know 'yourself" *in* your work; know what you do, so you can do what you know. Give shape to what you do; give it form by starting from mere instinct, from tradition, from convention, from routine, from *empeiria* [experience] and *tribē* [habituation] in order to arrive at 'self-conscious' action—a work in which you recognize yourself as the sole creator and actor."[40] Inherent in Cassirer's idea of the work is the bringing together of what is other and disparate from oneself. It depends upon the ideal of harmony that is present in the philosophical apprehension of culture. For Cassirer culture is the individual writ large. Self-knowledge has this objective basis and although it requires self-introspection it is not simply self-introspection. The work is a product of subjectivity but as its product it is something objective, something entered into culture by the individual. The work, then, is the product of human freedom understood as a form of self-determination. It cannot be and is not a result of instinct.

This ideal of self-knowledge is pluralistic and implies a doctrine of pluralistic philosophical inquiry, a doctrine that Cassirer practices in formulating his philosophy of symbolic forms. As Cassirer says in his preface to *An Essay on Man*: "It is my serious wish not to impose a ready-made theory, expressed in a dogmatic style, upon the minds of my readers. I have been anxious to place them in a position to judge for themselves."[41] For Cassirer, to philosophize rightly requires three things: (1) to consider what has been said before in the history of philosophy on the topic at hand, (2) to develop what can be said of it through a critical assessment of what other contemporary philosophers hold, and (3) to ground these philosophical views in the results of other fields of study that have bearing on the topic.

---

39. Bayer, *Cassirer's Metaphysics*, chap. 4.
40. Cassirer, *Philosophy of Symbolic Forms*, 4:186.
41. Cassirer, *Essay on Man*, 41.

Conclusion

This threefold way of proceeding is a large order but one that Cassirer shares with seminal pluralist thinkers such as James and Dewey, and with much of process philosophy. Cassirer saw philosophy as something ongoing, cooperative, and synthetic. He could agree with A. N. Whitehead, "A new idea introduces a new alternative; and we are not less indebted to a thinker when we adopt the alternative which he discarded."[42] Anything less than this for Cassirer would cut off inquiry. He saw the philosophy of symbolic forms as a project that was more grounded in questions than in arguments.

Philosophy must ultimately have a relation to the world. It is this ideal of bringing philosophy into human life and human culture that keeps philosophy open and honest. This ideal supports by its very nature a pluralist framework of mind for it does not allow philosophy to retreat into itself, there to foster an exclusive sense of reality and truth. This tendency for philosophy to withdraw from the world is anti-Socratic on Cassirer's view and therefore against philosophy's own origins as grounded in the pursuit of self-knowledge, the pursuit of which Cicero said "Socrates was the first to call philosophy down from the heavens and set her in the cities of men and bring her also into their homes and compel her to ask questions about life and morality and things good and evil."[43] Cassirer begins to ask the moral questions in *The Myth of the State* but this pursuit that has its roots in his earlier work was cut short by his sudden death and that appeared posthumously.

As discussed earlier, Cassirer endorses Schweitzer's view that philosophy cannot change the world directly but it can be the "watchman" who can tell us what the world is and what its possibilities are.[44] Cassirer's manner of philosophizing often seems to keep the world at too great an epistemological distance. Despite the intellectualism of his approach, Cassirer intends his philosophy to uphold this sense of the watchman who can attempt to command our attention and can place in our hands an ideal of human culture as a harmony of the forms of human activity and intelligence. And if this stance seems even yet too passive a role for philosophy, Cassirer would be the first to urge the philosopher to become a fellow worker and formulate the further role of philosophy's relation to the world.

---

42. Whitehead, *Process and Reality*, 16.
43. Cicero, *Tusculan Disputations*, 5.4.10.
44. Cassirer, *Symbol, Myth, and Culture*, 60.

Finally, we might ask, what are the implications of philosophical pluralism for human education? Since the *elenchos* of Socrates, the fundamental device of philosophical inquiry has been the question, with its answer being the result of reason. This process requires an openness to alternative points of view and a willingness to take human reason wherever it leads. This same openness of inquiry is the key to human learning. Without it, learning is a matter of authority and tradition acting alone. The ultimate authority in philosophical inquiry, and inquiry generally, is reason. And any claim to authority in the process of inquiry must also claim that such authority is supported by reason.

Philosophical idealism has often tended quite naturally toward monism over pluralism, hence James' above-mentioned charge against it of the "block universe." The dedication of philosophical idealism to the ideal that the True is the whole, an ideal that it can share with the concept of general education, as will be discussed in Chapter 8, inclines its manner of philosophizing toward a comprehensive account of experience. But having shown that such idealism is compatible with pluralism, as found in this chapter, a standard of openness of inquiry is set that can support such a principle in human education. If such an ideal can be pursued philosophically, taking the whole to be the object of reason, it can also be pursued educationally, taking the whole of human studies to be the object in the education of the individual. The pursuit of the whole cycle of human knowledge can be the aim of education and it can be such without limiting the ideal of openness endorsed in the outlook of pluralism.

5

The Phenomenology of Spirit as *Bildungsroman*

Rhetoric and Dialectic

As discussed at the beginning of this work, the German concept of *Bildung* is the education of the whole person. This understanding of education is based on the principle that the freedom of the individual is tied to the individual's power of self-determination. Self-determination is self-development so that the individual takes on an inner form, conceived as a dialectic of the self with its own reality. This dialectic is not simply a set of logical movements. It is also a matter of rhetoric, of the self expressing itself to itself as a being in the world. Hegel's *Phenomenology of Spirit* (*Geist*) is this self-determination writ large. It is the ultimate document of *Bildung* and hence is a philosophical version of the literary form of *Bildungsroman*.

In this chapter, I wish to explore the dimensions of the *Bildung* of the human spirit (*Geist*) as found in Hegel's masterpiece. In the manner of Plato's *Republic* of seeing in large letters what we may wish to see in small letters, we may in Hegel's dialectic of *Geist* itself see something of the *Geist* of the individual self as it folds itself back upon itself.

Although Hegel's absolute idealism is not pluralistic in the sense of pluralism as explored in the previous chapter, it displays an unexpected dimension of philosophical thought that is connected to the way in which philosophical ideas can be received and accepted. All philosophies have a rhetorical dimension that allows their readers to have access to them. Hegel's philosophy is no exception and if the dialectic of Hegel's system can be seen as connected to rhetoric, it is likely that other philosophies less comprehensive in scope can even more easily be seen in rhetorical terms.

Aristotle in the famous first line of his *Rhetoric* defines the relationship between rhetoric and dialectic: "Rhetoric is the counterpart of dialectic."[1] Both rhetoric and dialectic belong to no definitive science. They treat those things that come within the purview of all human beings. As an *antistrophes* to dialectic, rhetoric concerns particular cases and "its function is not simply to succeed in persuasion, but rather to discover the persuasive facts in each case."[2] Dialectic concerns reasoning on general issues and in its generality it is like deduction. But unlike deductive demonstration, dialectic, as Aristotle says in *Topics*, "reasons from reputable opinions," rather than from premises that are true and primitive.[3]

Kant in the *Critique of Pure Reason* takes a more extreme view of dialectic than Aristotle. Kant regards dialectic as a logic of illusion (*Schein*) that occurs when reason takes its powers beyond experience to make claims concerning the nature of the soul, world, and God. When reason attempts to determine the nature of what the soul is in itself, its assertions end in paralogisms; when it does so about the world its claims end in antinomies; and when it does so about God its efforts end in the impossibilities of the ontological, cosmological, and teleological arguments. Kant regards rhetoric as having no role in the philosophical pursuit of truth. In the *Critique of Judgment* Kant classifies rhetoric (*Beredsamkeit*) as belonging to fine art. He regards *ars oratoria* as an art of manipulation and deception that achieves its end by a beautiful show (*Schein*) of speech that plays upon human weaknesses. He says oratory deserves no respect whatsoever—"*ist gar keiner Achtung würdig*".[4] Kant's exclusion of rhetoric from *Kritik* (with which he identifies philosophy) establishes the general exclusion of rhetoric in the development of philosophical idealism.

Hegel interpretation for a century and a half presumed that rhetoric was irrelevant to understanding Hegel's thought. It considered Hegel's dialectic as a method independent of any connection to rhetoric. The first book on Hegel in English, James Hutchinson Stirling's *The Secret of Hegel*, published in 1863, regards the key to Hegel's system as his formulation of the concrete universal (*Begriff*). He makes no reference to rhetoric as an element in Hegel's thought.[5] In his preface to the *Phenomenology of*

---

1. Aristotle, *Rhetoric*, 1345b.
2. Ibid., 1355b.
3. Aristotle, *Topics*, 100a.
4. Kant, *Critique of Judgment*, 172n50.
5. Stirling, *Secret of Hegel*, xxii.

Spirit, Hegel mentions Plato's *Parmenides* as "surely the greatest artistic achievement of the ancient dialectic" but he makes no mention of rhetoric.⁶ A ground for ignoring rhetoric as important for Hegel's philosophy is the fact that Hegel himself ignores it. There is no discussion of rhetoric (*Redekunst*) in his whole corpus beyond a few pages concerning the differences between poetry and prose in his *Lectures on Fine Art*.⁷

All of the approaches to Hegel in non-rhetorical terms changed with the appearance of Donald Phillip Verene, *Hegel's Recollection: A Study of Images in the "Phenomenology of Spirit"* followed by John H. Smith, *The Spirit and Its Letter: Traces of Rhetoric in Hegel's Philosophy of "Bildung."* Verene's work showed that there is a dialectic between image (*Bild*) and concept (*Begriff*) within Hegel's mode of expression that provides the reader with a necessary means of access to the work. Smith's study showed not only that Hegel employs rhetorical principles in the composition of the *Phenomenology* but that Hegel in his early years studied rhetoric closely and was concerned to master it. Smith's work, although developed independently of Verene's, joined with it to present a new reading of Hegel. This poetical and rhetorical grasp of Hegel's thought has been recently restated in Verene's *Hegel's Absolute*.

My views that follow begin where Verene's and Smith's accounts leave off. I wish to consider two questions that extend what has been broached in their readings of Hegel. First, in what sense does Hegel's *Phenomenology* embody a transformation of the Aristotelian conception of rhetoric as an *antistrophes* to dialectic? Second, to what extent does the Hegelian connection of dialectic to rhetoric suggest a sense of the sublime, especially as found in Longinus' *Peri Hypsos* (*On the Sublime*)? My aim in pursuing these two questions is not to produce a historical interpretation of Hegel's *Phenomenology* but to extract its unique embodiment of philosophical rhetoric. My analysis is confined to the *Phenomenology* taking it as Hegel understood it as the first part of his system and the schema of movement for the second part of the system in the *Science of Logic*.⁸ The dialectical and rhetorical use of images certainly extends throughout Hegel's later works from the "bad infinity" (*Schlecht-Unendliche*) in the *Science of Logic* to the famous "owl of Minerva" metaphor in the preface to the *Philosophy of Right*, but the comprehension of these and how these works may differ

---

6. Hegel, *Phenomenology*, 71.

7. Hegel, *Aesthetics*, 2:986–95.

8. Hegel, *Science of Logic*, 28–29.

in rhetorical terms from the earlier *Phenomenology* is a project that passes beyond the bounds of these remarks.

Ars Critica and Ars Topica

Two forces bear down on Hegel's formulation of the *Phenomenology*: the attachment of the Enlightenment or *Aufklärung* to reason as an instrument of criticism and the reaction of the Romantic movement to it that originates in the last three decades of the eighteenth century. Hegel's philosophy takes shape from the statement of *The Earliest System-Program of German Idealism* of 1796–97 through the *Kritisches Journal der Philosophie* announced by Hegel and Schelling in 1801 to the Jena writings of the *Systementwürfe* especially the lecture manuscript for the *Realphilosophie* of 1805–6 just before the publication of the *Phenomenology* in 1807. *The Earliest System-Program* advocates the need for "a mythology of reason [*eine Mythologie der Vernunft*]," an ideal that goes on to inform Hegel's employment of images in the *Phenomenology*.[9]

Hegel rejects the *Aukklärung's* dedication to *Kritik* that culminates in Kant's conception of the Understanding (*Verstand*). The assertion of *ars critica* and rejection of *ars topica* has its origin in the *Port-Royal Logic* of Antoine Arnauld and Pierre Nicole of 1662. The *Port-Royal Logic* never explicitly attacks the *ars topica*; it simply replaces it by distinguishing between two senses of method—one called *analysis* or *method of resolution or invention* and the other called *synthesis* or *method of composition or doctrine*. The former is used for the discovery of the truth and the latter for making it understandable.[10] The former is essentially the Cartesian step-by-step method of right reasoning in the sciences. This conception of logic eliminates that of the *Topics*, which is connected to Aristotle's original *Organon* that is part of Aristotle's twofold sense of the syllogism. One of these is the rhetorical sense of the syllogism, which acts as the means for the formation of arguments based on what the Latins called the art of finding the middle term (*terminus medius*), the term that would be most accepted by an audience to link successfully the two terms of the conclusion. The other is the purely deductive sense of the syllogism tied to the rules for evaluating the validity of the syllogism once formed.

---

9. Hegel, "Systemprogramm," 236.
10. Arnaud and Nicole, *La logique*, 299.

Moral Philosophy and Moral Education

A further ground of the Enlightenment is the pyrrhonism of Pierre Bayle's *Dictionnaire historique et critique* of 1695, which shows reason to be an instrument with which critically to assess arguments and evidence on all subjects throughout experience and to sort out truth from error and illusion. Bayle's skepticism stands as a precursor to the great *L'Encyclopédie* of universal knowledge of Diderot and d'Alembert of 1751–76. Hegel's counter to this Enlightenment conception of knowledge as based on *raisonnement* is the title he gave to the manual from which he taught his system—*The Encyclopedia of Philosophical Sciences in Outline*, which is the summary of his conception of speculative science.

Kant is the culmination of the Enlightenment fascination with criticism by turning the critical power of reason back upon itself. Kant says: "Our age is, in especial degree, the age of criticism [*Zeitalter der Kritik*], and to criticism everything must submit."[11] In accord with this assessment Kant says he wishes "to institute a tribunal which will assure to reason its lawful claims, and dismiss all groundless pretensions, not by despotic decrees, but in accordance with its own eternal and unalterable laws. This tribunal is no other than the *critique of pure reason*." In so doing Kant declares that he does not intend a critique of books and systems "but of the faculty of reason in general, in respect of all knowledge after which it may strive *independently of all experience*."[12]

Kant's transcendental logic allows for a legitimate use of reason as analytic of experience that is reminiscent of the *Port-Royal* dedication to the analytic method of resolution. The logic that Kant follows to derive the table of categories in the *Critique of Pure Reason* is Georg Friedrich Meier's logic, the *Vernunftlehre* of 1752. Kant's conception of transcendental logic has no place for topics. All uses of reason that go beyond experience constitute a logic of illusion or dialectic. In place of topics Kant offers regulative ideas that, while not constitutive of experience, can be entrusted to the mind as general guides to its reasonings about experience.

Kritik for Hegel is rhetorically propaedeutic to his sense of philosophy.[13] It is tied to reflection as the basis of philosophical thought. Hegel says that reflection became a slogan (*Schlagwort*) of modern philosophy so that "*reflective* understanding took possession of philosophy."[14] Kant's

---

11. Kant, *Critique of Pure Reason*, 9 note.
12. Ibid.
13. Smith, *Spirit and Its Letter*, chap. 3.
14. Hegel, *Science of Logic*, 43.

"transcendental reflection" is the prime example of this slogan of reflection. Hegel, as will be discussed, wishes to overcome the Enlightenment's limitation of philosophy to critical reflection and to regain the ancient conception of philosophy as speculation. Hegel in the *Phenomenology* intends reflection to be superseded (*aufgehoben*) in his conception of speculation.

The other standpoint that Hegel intends to be *aufgehoben* in the *Phenomenology* is the affirmation of the self and the value of individual experience present in the developing Romantic movement. This sense of individual experience has its roots in Rousseau's *Julie, ou la nouvelle Héloïse* of 1761 and is found in Goethe's *The Sorrows of Young Werther* of 1774 and the verse dramas of Schiller such as *The Robbers* of 1781. Hegel intends to overcome the limitations of the Romantics' extreme sense of the cultivation of the self with his concept of *Bildung*. Hegel says that "the individual has the right to demand that Science [*Wissenschaft*] should at least provide him with the ladder to this standpoint [that of *Wissenschaft*], should show him this standpoint within himself."[15] The *Phenomenology* is an account of the systematic development of the self itself and has been rightly called a philosophical *Bildungsroman*, the roots of which are in the literary versions of self-education in Wieland's *Agathon* of 1765–66 and Goethe's *Wilhelm Meisters Lehrjahr* of 1795–96.

Hegel's dialectic is not the logic of illusion that occurs when reason goes beyond the bounds of the analysis of experience into a metaphysical Aether. Hegel's dialectic is the key to a new science of science—"the science of the experience of consciousness [*Wissenschaft der Erfahrung des Bewußtseins*]."[16] By means of this science the human self systematically develops itself through stages of experience to the point of grasping experience as a whole—the point of "absolute knowing." The Romantics' absoluteness of the individual self is transformed into the self's absolute grasp of its own being. The Romantics' absoluteness of the emotions is taken over by an absolute of reason. The Romantics' view of poesy as an *Ursprache* is incorporated into Hegel's conception of *Bildung*. Hegel calls poesy the "Instructress of Humankind [*Lehrerin der Menschheit*]."[17]

Hegel's speculative sense of dialectic in the *Phenomenology* has behind it a new sense of topics that makes each stage of the development of consciousness possible. Once Kant bases his philosophy on *Kritik*, he can

---

15. Hegel, *Phenomenology*, 26.
16. Ibid., 88.
17. Hegel, "Systemprogramm," 235.

never recover the art of topics that makes possible the generation of experience. He can offer an analytic account of the possibility of experience but he cannot offer a topical account. In the final chapter of the *Phenomenology* on "Absolute Knowing" Hegel claims that the science of the experience of consciousness is a memory theater. His science is accompanied by an art of memory (*Erinnerung*) and this art produces a Gallery of Images (*Galerie von Bildern*).[18] This is in accord with the Renaissance art of memory as described by Frances Yates in *The Art of Memory*.[19] The memory is a treasure house of master images from which we can draw forth the dialectical stages of experience. These images are, so to speak, the middle terms of experience from which all *argumenta* or themes of consciousness can be entertained. They are the *topoi* or *loci*—the commonplaces—that hold consciousness together at its base. The *Phenomenology* gives us an order of these topics arranged as stages from sense-certainty to self-certainty to the certainty of reason and spirit through which consciousness can develop in order finally to achieve a grasp of the principle that: "The True is the whole [*Das Wahre ist das Ganze*]."[20] How does Hegel accomplish this result?

The Double *Ansich*

The fundamental problem in the development of German idealism is how to comprehend being-in-itself (*das Ansichsein*). Kant's solution to this problem is his famous distinction between the "thing-in-itself" (*Ding-an-sich*) and the thing as phenomenal object. The thing is knowable only to the extent it appears to the knower. Its reality in itself is closed to cognition and is noumenal. Once Kant declares the *Ding-an-sich* to be unknowable, he can claim that the knower by reflecting on the knower's own act of knowing determines the conditions of possibility for how the phenomenal object is known. The knower has unimpeded access to the conditions of the knower's own activity. Knowledge of these conditions, then, is the product of "transcendental reflection." Such reflection can articulate the workings of the Understanding. Should the knower attempt to extend the power of reflection to attain a knowledge of the thing-in-itself, this attempt would transcend the bounds of experience. The knower would be unable to produce a sensible intuition with which to schematize a concept. Such

---

18. Hegel, *Phenomenology*, 808.
19. Yates, *Art of Memory*, chaps. 1–2.
20. Hegel, *Phenomenology*, 20.

transcendent (as opposed to transcendental) reflection can produce only a dialectic of metaphysical opinions concerning the thing-in-itself with no basis in experience to resolve the oppositions inherent in such opinions.

Kant extols the merits of limiting cognition to the domain of the pure Understanding (*Verstand*): "This domain is an island, enclosed by nature itself within unalterable limits. It is the land of truth—enchanting name!—surrounded by a wide and stormy ocean, the native home of illusion, where many a fog bank and many a swiftly melting iceberg give the deceptive appearance of farther shores, deluding the adventurous seafarer ever anew with empty hopes, and engaging him in enterprises which he can never abandon and yet is unable to carry to completion."[21] The Understanding is the land of truth in which thought through its power of *Kritik* focuses on the principles of its knowledge of experience and keeps itself from overstepping the bounds of experience. Within experience *Kritik* will provide us a means to distinguish truth from error and our success in this process will prevent us from any adventures pure reason may urge us to undertake.

Hegel's philosophy is nothing but adventure (*Abenteuer*). Speculation is intellectual and spiritual adventure. Hegelian idealism begins in the realization that the distinction between the phenomenal object and the noumenal object is a distinction that thought creates for itself. This realization is coupled with what Hegel calls "determinate negation"—that all truths are partial truths and that what is outside a given truth—what the truth negates—has specific content.[22] This content plays a necessary role in the nature of what the truth determines. Kant's system is a structure of static distinctions and distinctions within distinctions that define experience. Within Kant's critical analytic, nothing truly moves. Above all, we do not even know from its perspective how the phenomenal object arises from the noumenal.

Hegel resolves the problem of the in-itself by applying dialectic (which Kant keeps outside experience) within experience. Hegel makes experience itself dialectical. To do this Hegel replaces the reflective sentence, which affirms and denies connections between classes of objects, with the speculative sentence (*spekulativer Satz*).[23] In so doing Hegel passes beyond the Understanding (*Verstand*), the faculty of reflection, to Reason (*Vernunft*), the native home of speculation. He says the Understanding yields only a

21. Kant, *Critique of Pure Reason*, 257.
22. Hegel, *Phenomenology*, 79.
23. Ibid., 59–65.

table of contents of experience: "A table of contents is all that it offers, the content itself it does not offer at all."²⁴

Reason is the inner life of experience. The speculative sentence is the primary device of reason. In the speculative sentence the copula achieves not simply a static connection between the subject and predicate but a dynamic or dialectical movement. In the speculative sentence the subject at first appears to contain the essence of what is asserted, but when we attempt to affirm this of the subject we find this essence to be expressed in the predicate. The predicate says what the subject is. Yet when we attempt to affirm this of the predicate, we find the predicate has meaning only in its connection to the subject. When we return to the subject through the predicate, we confront a transformed sense of the subject as its meaning now inherently contains what it is in terms of the predicate. The speculative sentence is internally dialectical. The reflective sentence of class logic simply ignores this internal dialectical movement that actually holds the sentence together.

Hegel begins his *Phenomenology* by placing Kant's "thing-in-itself" into a dialectical relation to the "thing-as-it-is-for-us." In the introduction to his work Hegel claims that consciousness moves from its apprehension of its object as something "in-itself" (*ansich*) to the apprehension of this in-itself as something for us or, so to speak, something "for-itself" (*fürsich*). We are aware of the object before us and then we are aware of our awareness of it. The two moments are different in kind yet they can exist only because of their mutual dependence. When we move from the second moment back to the first, the first becomes a new in-itself. In this new in-itself the original in-itself is *aufgehoben*, that is, the original in-itself has been cancelled and transcended but at the same time something of it has been preserved and transformed in a new actuality.

Hegel says that "Upon this distinction [that between the two moments], which is present as a fact, the examination [*Prüfung*] rests."²⁵ Verene calls this movement between the two moments "the double *Ansich*."²⁶ He points out that no major Hegel scholar subscribes to the mistaken popular view that Hegel's dialectic is triadic, a movement of thesis-antithesis-synthesis. At no place in his corpus does Hegel describe his dialectic by putting these three terms together. In the introduction to the *Phenomenology*, Hegel de-

---

24. Ibid., 53.
25. Ibid., 85.
26. Verene, *Hegel's Absolute*, chap. 2.

scribes his method as a double movement of *an-und-für-sich-sein*. The *und* (and) does not signify a synthesis; it designates the connection described above. Hegel, in fact, attributes a triadic form of philosophizing to Kant and calls it a "lifeless schema."[27]

Hegel, like Kant, connects dialectic with illusion, but, unlike Kant, Hegel's illusion lies not outside experience but within it. Each stage of the development of consciousness in Hegel's *Phenomenology* is based on an illusion—the illusion that consciousness has accomplished a synthesis of its two moments and overcome the "andness" that separates them. As each stage presses itself to realize this synthesis it collapses from within and must make a new beginning for itself in a new stage that will also meet the same fate. Hegel thus calls the progression of stages "a highway of despair [*Weg der Verzweiflung*]."[28] Hegel says that in this progression consciousness repeatedly forgets itself and must find a new beginning. It is always learning something "but equally it is always forgetting it and starting the movement all over again [*und fängt die Bewegung von forne an*]."[29] The disputation between opinions that typifies the classical conception of dialectic is transformed by Hegel into a progression of "opinions," each one developed to the point of it giving way to a further one such that the total progression is a system of human experience itself.

Absolute knowing as understood through the theory of the double *Ansich* is not a final synthesis of all the stages of consciousness into a unified whole. Instead it is precisely the realization by consciousness that all of its prior attempts at synthesis are specific forms of illusion. Absolute knowing is ultimate human wisdom—the acceptance of things as they are. The two moments of consciousness can be realized in various ways and can be comprehended as a totality—as a *coincidentia oppositorum* dialectically developed. The two moments, while different in kind, nonetheless require each other but they do not disappear into each other. Absolute knowing is a melancholy wisdom that leads to the *Science of Logic*, the problem of which is to show to what extent these phenomenal forms can be apprehended as a system of metaphysical thoughts.

---

27. Hegel, *Phenomenology*, 50.
28. Ibid., 78.
29. Ibid., 109.

Sublime Science

We have at this point a picture of how Hegel transforms dialectic from the classical method of disputation drawing arguments from common opinion into a method through which consciousness achieves a form of self-knowledge—a philosophical *Bildungsroman*. If rhetoric is the counterpart of dialectic, is there a corresponding transformation of rhetoric in the Hegelian system?

Hegel's dialectic, like dialectic in general, deals with the universal. The stages of the *Phenomenology* are the universal forms of human experience, of the human self as it comes to a grasp of itself through the power of reason. Such is Hegel's science. But this science must be conveyed in a particular speech, one that can persuade its audience of its reasonings. Hegel's speech is unique. It might be said of Hegel as it is said of a line of Shakespeare that one can no more steal a line of Hegel than steal the club of Hercules. In contrast to Kant's Latinized German and his often Scholastic manner of making distinctions, Hegel's language is Socratic. Hegel has no truly technical vocabulary; he attempts to create a new *agora* from German as a natural language. In a well-known letter of May 1805 to Johann Heinrich Voss, the translator of Homer into German, Hegel wrote, "Luther made the Bible, you have made Homer speak German . . . I wish to attempt to teach philosophy to speak German."[30]

Hegel's work is full of wordplays that go to the root meanings of the words of ordinary German and bring forth the philosophical significance in them. The opening of the *Phenomenology* centers on a pun on *Meinung* as the word for opinion (verb: *meinen*, to opine) that contains the possessive adjective, mine (*mein*)—an opinion is mine, something peculiar to an individual—*nach meiner Meinung*, in my opinion. I attempt to grasp the object as mine because my senses make me certain of it. I attempt to possess it like an opinion. The next stage plays on the German word for perception—*Wahrnehmung*. The verb *wahrnehmen* is literally "to take for true" (*wahr*, true; *nehmen*, to take). Hegel claims that when I give up on my attempt to possess the object in its immediacy, "I take the truth of it [*nehme ich wahr*]."[31] The object then becomes for me a thing having its own substance.

---

30. Hegel, *Briefe*, 1:99–100.
31. Hegel, *Phenomenology*, 110.

Hegel quite consciously plays on the root meaning of his central term of *Begriff*, which does not translate well into the Latin-based term *concept* (*conceptus*). The Latin root has the sense of collection or gathering. *Begriff* preserves the meaning of grasping (verb: *greifen*, to grasp, seize, catch hold of; *begreifen*, to comprehend or grasp mentally). Along with *Begriff*, one of Hegel's most important terms is *Aufhebung* (verb: *aufheben*), which as mentioned earlier refers to the way in which the transitions between stages of consciousness occur. Hegel explicitly plays on the double sense of this ordinary German word meaning both to cancel something and at the same time to preserve it. There is likely a play on *fahren*, to travel, that lies within the word for experience, *Erfahrung* (verb: *erfahren*, to come to know, experience, suffer, undergo). Consciousness travels the highway of despair (*der Weg der Verzweiflung*) in its formation of experience. To travel is to be on a *Weg* and to encounter any of the perils or joys that lie on it.

In his use of *Erinnerung* or recollection as a key term to describe absolute knowing at the end of the *Phenomenology*, Hegel hyphenates it as *Er-innerung* to emphasize its sense of inwardness.[32] Hegel's "doubleness" of thought requires a "doubleness" of expression. Rather than reducing words to single, conceptual meanings as is the aim of reflection and the Understanding, Hegel preserves the ambiguities in his major terms and exploits the metaphorical and ironic power contained in these ambiguities and root meanings to coin a unique philosophical voice.

Hegel's science (*Wissenschaft*) is a linguistic and rhetorically based science that produces a systematic way of speaking about experience. Smith says: "Hegel's philosophical conception of the development of knowledge cannot be separated from the development of modes of representation. Both the universal and the individual Spirit attain knowledge only by retracing a history of self-representations. *Wissenschaft* is thereby tied to the key rhetorical principle of *elocution*."[33] It is a sublime science in both the Kantian and the classical sense of Longinus.

Kant in the *Critique of Judgment* analyzes a sense of the "mathematically sublime (*Mathematisch-Erhabenen*). Kant claims that for the purely mathematical estimation of magnitude there is no maximum but that for aesthetic estimation of it there is always a maximum. Of this second sense of maximum he says, "if it is judged as the absolute measure than which no greater is possible subjectively (for the judging subject), it brings with

---

32. Ibid., 808.
33. Smith, *Spirit and Its Letter*, 177.

it the idea of the sublime and produces that emotion which no mathematical estimation by means of numbers can bring about...."[34] One of Kant's examples is St. Peter's at Rome. He says that for the spectator who enters St. Peter's Square, "there is here a feeling of the inadequacy of his imagination for presenting the ideas of a whole, wherein the imagination reaches its maximum, and, in striving to surpass it, sinks back into itself...."[35] Kant has in mind both made and natural objects in experience that cannot be taken in aesthetically. They go beyond what the spectator's imagination can encompass.

Hegel's Absolute in the *Phenomenology* is an intellectual sublime. In the *Lectures on Fine Art*, Hegel says, "The sublime in general is the attempt to express the infinite, without finding in the sphere of phenomena an object which proves adequate for this representation. Precisely because the infinite is set apart from the entire complex of objectivity as explicitly an invisible meaning devoid of shape and is made inner, it remains, in accordance with its infinity, unutterable and sublime above any expression through the finite."[36]

In the final pages of the *Phenomenology*, Hegel describes the various aspects of the self-knowledge of spirit as it externalizes itself as nature and then returns from this externalization to reinstate itself as subject.[37] But Hegel is never able to produce the Absolute as a phenomenon. When consciousness is at the limit of the totality of the shapes of experience, it has passed beyond them. The Absolute is not a standpoint of consciousness but is consciousness itself. This standpoint is unutterable. Thus Hegel closes his work by his gloss on two lines of Schiller's poem, *Die Freundschaft*: "from the chalice of this realm of spirits/ foams forth for Him his own infinitude."[38]

Hegel ends the science of the experience of consciousness with a master image of the sublime. It is an image of the deity whose being is realized in the infinitude of the deity's creation. Yet the forms (spirits, *Geister*) are always on the verge of outstripping the infinite of their creator's infinitude. It is a masterful vision that persuades Hegel's reader of the sublime

---

34. Kant, *Critique of Judgment*, 89–90.
35. Ibid., 91.
36. Hegel, *Aesthetics*, 1:363.
37. Hegel, *Phenomenology*, 807.
38. Ibid., 808.

stance of his Absolute, a whole that cannot be completed but must forever be recollected in the attempt at completion.

Longinus distinguishes five senses of the sublime in literature. He says that "the first and most powerful is the power of grand conceptions ... and the second is the inspiration of vehement emotion."[39] Hegel's conception of the True as the whole and that this is present in the Absolute is one of the grandest and most sublime conceptions in the history of philosophy. This conception is coupled with the extraordinary passion of his text in which he declares that: "The True is the Bacchanalian revel in which no member is not drunk."[40] He dismissed the formalistic or non-dialectical philosophy of nature as mere "pigeon-holing," offering up the living organism of nature as "a synoptic table like a skeleton with scraps of paper stuck all over it."[41] He dismisses the view that the Absolute is an identity of A=A, that is, an Absolute in which there is only simple identity with no internal order.[42]

In his discussion of the pseudo-science of phrenology, he characterizes its adherents as essentially deadheads and in the one place in the *Phenomenology* where Hegel becomes violent he speaks of beating in the skulls of phrenologists: "the retort here would, strictly speaking, have to go to the length of beating in the skull of anyone making such a judgment [claiming that the reality of the individual is revealed by the shape of the skull]."[43] Finally he says the "scientific thinking" of the phrenologists is nothing more than a kind of mental urination, making a pun on *Wissen* (knowing) and *Pissen* (pissing).[44] At the end of the *Phenomenology*, Hegel plays upon a second and profound sense of the skull—Golgotha (*Schädelstätte*)—the place of the crucifixion and uses the phrase the "Calvary [or Golgotha] of absolute Spirit [*Geist*]" to describe the *Phenomenology* itself.[45] This is not only passionate speech, the subject matter is the passionate condition of spirit.

Longinus says that these first two sources of the sublime are "for the most part congenital," but the other three "come partly from art." The third and fourth sources involve the nobility of language achieved in figures of

---

39. Longinus, *Sublime*, 8.1.
40. Hegel, *Phenomenology*, 47.
41. Ibid., 51.
42. Ibid., 16.
43. Ibid., 339.
44. Ibid., 346.
45. Ibid., 808. See Verene, *Hegel's Recollection*, 88–91.

speech and figures of thought. They concern the "choice of words and the use of metaphor and elaborated diction."[46] The fifth source, Longinus says, which "gives form to all those already mentioned, is dignified and elevated word-arrangement." In making a transition from his discussion of the first two sources of sublimity to figures of speech and thought, Longinus says that "weight, grandeur, and urgency in writing" are very largely produced by the use of *phantasiai* or images. He says these are passages in which "you seem to see what you describe and bring it vividly before the eyes of your audience."[47]

The *Phenomenology* is structured around such images. Hegel establishes an internal dialectic in his text between *Bild* (image) and *Begriff* in which the reader is given access through the *Bild* to the *Begriff*. Hegel's figures of speech are dialectically connected to his figures of thought. We are able to recollect the text of the *Phenomenology* in terms of our absorption of its master images such as the inverted world, the unhappy consciousness, the master and servant, the beautiful soul, and the spiritual zoo or animal kingdom. Once we experience these images at Hegel's hand they remain in our memory and are topics from which we can always take ourselves back to the dialectical forms they contain. Longinus says that the truly sublime text has an effect on our sensibility such that we return to it many times: "For what is truly great bears repeated consideration; it is difficult, nay, impossible, to resist its effect; and the memory of it is stubborn and indelible."[48]

The one figure of thought that is never explicitly stated that dominates the whole of the *Phenomenology* is that of the journey, the descent, and the homecoming. The *Phenomenology* is Homer's *Odyssey*, Vergil's *Aeneid*, the Stations of the Cross, Dante's *Divine Comedy*. The Absolute is Ithaca in which consciousness comes full circle. It is Aeneas' descent into the underworld with the golden bough (his dialectic) where from Anchises he learns his future, the beginning and the end. It is the Via Dolorosa, the route from Pilate's tribunal to Golgotha. It is Dante's entrance into the dark wood of error, his descent, ascent, and arrival back into the world. The archetype of the journey dominates Hegel's philosophical *Bildungsroman*.

Longinus likens the fifth source of sublimity—the organization of the work—to that of the human body. He says: "None of the members has any

---

46. Longinus, *Sublime*, 8.1.
47. Ibid., 15.1.
48. Ibid., 7.3.

value by itself apart from the others, yet one with another they all constitute a perfect system." He claims further that if the parts "are united into a single whole and embraced by the bonds of rhythm, then they gain a living voice just by being merely rounded into a period."[49] Hegel's above-mentioned principle that the "True is the whole" applies to the nature of the work in which his assertion of this principle occurs. Hegel intends to have given the complete speech. If there is anything left to say, it can find a place within what has already been said.

The reader might complain that Hegel is hard to read, that the paragraphs are too long, and that they often contain inelegant sentences. Indeed, the *Phenomenology* is commonly regarded as the most difficult book to read in the history of philosophy. But the work, once grasped, comes forth as a grand whole, a unique intellectual narrative. It is, however, not a journey everyone can make, not a quest everyone can undertake. Hegel in his preface informs the reader that philosophical truth is not to be had in summaries and simple statements. In one of his most famous metaphors—that of the shoemaker—he writes: "there seems to be a currently prevailing prejudice to the effect that, although not everyone who has eyes and fingers, and is given leather and last, is at once in a position to make shoes, everyone nevertheless immediately understands how to philosophize, and how to evaluate philosophy, since he possesses the criterion for doing so in his natural reason—as if he did not likewise possess the measure for a shoe in his own foot."[50]

Rhetoric as Philosophy

Hegel's rhetoric is a counterpart to his dialectic. He persuades the reader by a totalizing mode of expression that conveys many things at once and that exploits the ambiguities of natural language. None of what Hegel says is achieved by individual arguments or philosophical proofs. The reader is confronted with a dialectic that draws the reader into the movement of consciousness itself. The images upon which this movement depends enter the reader's memory and become the basis for the reader to grasp Hegel's system.

Ernesto Grassi, in a brief article on Hegel's *The Earliest System-Program of German Idealism*, connects Hegel's call for a "mythology of

---

49. Ibid., 40.1.
50. Hegel, *Phenomenology*, 67.

reason" and claim that poetry is the "Instructress of Humankind," mentioned earlier, to the rhetorical tradition of Renaissance Humanism.[51] Grassi's remarks, influenced by Verene's interpretation of Hegel, extend to Hegel's early philosophy, the thesis he developed in *Rhetoric as Philosophy*, which appeared in its first edition in 1980. In this work, Grassi redefines rhetoric from a form of speech that is designed to persuade an audience of what has been independently established by theoretical and rationalistic means to a form of speech that gives us our original access to the world and upon which all ratiocinative thought depends. This original form of speech is metaphorical. Grassi says: "If the image, the metaphor, belongs to rhetorical speech . . . we also are obliged to recognize that every original, former, 'archaic' speech . . . cannot have a rational but only a rhetorical character." And he concludes: "Thus the term 'rhetoric' assumes a fundamentally new significance; 'rhetoric' is not, nor can it be the art, the technique of an exterior persuasion; it is rather the speech which is the basis of the rational thought."[52]

Grassi claims that first or primordial speech—that through which we make the world—is metaphorical; "the metaphor lies at the root of our human world."[53] Hegel understands this role of the metaphor in his claim that poesy is the teacher of all humanity—including the philosopher. Philosophy recreates experience through reason but its rational speech cannot be separated from the archaic speech upon which reason depends for the beginning points or *topoi*. Philosophy is without question rhetorical in form, but a particular kind of form that Hegel captures in his phrase "mythology of reason." As Grassi puts it: "The metaphor lies at the root of our knowledge in which rhetoric and philosophy attain their original unity. Therefore we cannot speak of rhetoric *and* philosophy, but every original philosophy is rhetoric and every true and not exterior rhetoric is philosophy."[54]

Conclusion

Grassi stresses that the metaphor is the product of the power of *ingenium*—the capacity to find the similarity in the dissimilar. There is no method for making metaphors. In the *Poetics* Aristotle says that to be a master of

51. Grassi, "Remarks on German Idealism," 125–33.
52. Grassi, *Rhetoric as Philosophy*, 20.
53. Ibid., 33.
54. Ibid., 34.

metaphor is the greatest thing by far, because "it is the one thing that cannot be learnt from others; and it is also a sign of genius, since a good metaphor implies an intuitive perception of the similarity in dissimilars."[55] The doubleness in the metaphor is the source of the doubleness of dialectic as the form of reason. The metaphor is inherently dialectical. Smith calls attention to Hegel's claim of the "doubleness" of metaphorical expression.[56] The metaphor with its sense of doubleness is always there at any true beginning point of thought. In the *Rhetoric* Aristotle claims: "Now strange words simply puzzle us; ordinary words convey only what we know already; it is from metaphor that we can best get hold of something fresh."[57]

The opposites of Hegel's dialectic are always developed in terms of something that they hold in common. The secret of Hegel, to recall Hutchinson Stirling's phrase, is *ingenium*. The True that is the whole rests on our ability to see all the aspects of experience as able to be articulated in terms of each other. Hegelian rhetoric takes us to the basis of what philosophical speech is. The reader of the *Phenomenology* can comprehend it only through the sufficient use of *ingenium*, otherwise Hegel's text remains a mystical treatise, an eclectic speech.

What are the implications of the phenomenology of spirit, rhetorically understood, for human education? Human education as well as philosophy since Socrates has had self-knowledge as its aim. Education as self-knowledge is understood as involving a total orientation of the individual's mind and spirit rather than the acquisition of some specific forms of knowledge. The phenomenology of spirit as advanced by Hegel presents the individual with a picture of self-knowledge writ large. It shows that development of human consciousness itself as a process of self-realization. All of the stages of this development are present both in human consciousness as such and in the individual consciousness as it seeks education in the sense of *Bildung*. Thus, Hegel's phenomenology can rightly be called a philosophical *Bildungsroman*.

Crucial to this process of self-knowledge or self-cultivation is rhetoric. Reason in its attempt to grasp experience as a whole cannot dispense with the tropes of thought that make ideas comprehensible. Human education cannot simply be the training of the mind in rational thought. It must also be the training of the tongue and heart. Clarity of thought is not enough.

---

55. Aristotle, *Poetics* 1459a.
56. Smith, *Spirit and Its Letter*, 180.
57. Aristotle, *Rhetoric*, 1410b.

The individual must acquire the principles by which ideas can be communicated. The fact that rhetorical tropes are required to make Hegelian philosophy comprehensible—a philosophy that is immersed in dialectical reason—demonstrates that rhetoric cannot be separated from the pursuit of rationality and from an education in the use of reason. Hegelian rhetoric becomes a kind of model for the comprehension of the human world as a whole, an ideal that can guide the cycle of studies that defines human education in its broadest sense.

6

Rhetoric and Human Education

Vico as Juristical Grammaticus

In the previous chapter, the role of rhetoric was examined as a crucial aspect of *Bildung* or the education of the whole person as found in Hegel's dialectical comprehension of experience. In what follows, I wish to carry this role of rhetoric in human education further by considering the views of Vico and, in doing so, to show the connection of human conduct with the distinctively human institution of law. From this perspective, law is regarded not as a body of restrictions placed upon the actions of the individual to prevent a Hobbesian "war of all against all" but as the repository of civil wisdom, the study of which gives the individual guidance in the formation of a moral self. The law in this sense is the ultimate basis of moral education and, in fact, of moral philosophy.

Vico's *On the Study Methods of Our Time* presents us with a complete theory of education formulated against Cartesianism. Descartes' conception of clarity and certainty in human knowledge precludes from it all those forms of thinking that are traditionally placed under the heading of civil wisdom. The humanities generally, including jurisprudence, depend upon reasoning that proceeds from common sense and tradition and provides us with well-turned probabilities, not logical certainties. The modern world and our conception of systems of education with it are Cartesian. The art of oratory, the art of memory, and the art of topics that have always been crucial for the study of jurisprudence are no longer a part of education. Is it possible to resurrect them? If it is, Vico is a key figure for so doing. In my remarks that follow I wish to focus on two questions: First, what is Vico's conception of rhetorical speech? And second, what implications does this conception have for education in the humanities and jurisprudence?

Moral Philosophy and Moral Education

There are two ways to learn pedagogy from Vico. One is to consider who Vico himself was, how he existed as a teacher and thinker. The other is to assemble into a single account his doctrine of humanistic education. My subject in this section is the first of these. The succeeding sections are concerned with the second, bringing together what Vico says in various of his works.

Vico was professor of Latin eloquence at the University of Naples, a position he held for over forty years from 1669 to 1741 (from age thirty-one to age seventy-three) when he was succeeded in his professorship by his son Gennaro. His principal duty was to prepare very young students to qualify in the law. His position also required him to deliver the oration that marked the beginning of the academic year. His above-mentioned oration of 1708 on the system or method of studies was the seventh of these (I will refer to it in the chapter as his seventh oration), the preceding six were also on various themes of education.[1] Beyond the succession of these first seven orations Vico delivered three further inaugural university orations. In one delivered in 1713, the full text of which is lost, Vico addressed the general theme of "how to make choice and use of the sciences for eloquence."[2] In another delivered in 1719, the full text of which is also lost, Vico presented the argument that "All divine and human learning has three elements: knowledge, will and power, whose single principle is the mind, with reason for its eye, to which God brings the light of eternal truth."[3] This oration is indirectly pedagogical. Most directly it presents the standpoint that underlies his three books of *Universal Law* that appeared in the 1720s.

Vico's final university oration was delivered in 1732, *De mente heroica*, "On the Heroic Mind." This oration is second in importance only to Vico's seventh oration of 1708. The theme of this later oration returns to that of the earlier one and adds to it the concept of the hero which Vico had developed in the intervening years in the two versions of his *New Science* (1725 and 1730). In the development of a nation the hero is the embodiment of the virtues that form the basis of civil life. But once the age of heroes is past in the course of a nation the heroic deeds upon which its customs are formed are no longer possible. In such a post-heroic age, an age of strictly human institutions (the age of modernity in which we and Vico live), heroism remains only as a way of thinking, as a stance of the mind, not as a form

---

1. Vico, *Humanistic Education*.
2. Vico, *Autobiography*, 125.
3. Ibid., 156.

of action. Elio Gianturco, the translator of the seventh oration, considers Vico's "On the Heroic Mind" as "one of the most inspired 'invitations to learning' ever penned.... The *erōs* of learning has seldom been expressed in more electrifying terms."[4]

Vico's use of "heroic" may have its source in Plato's *Cratylus* in which it is claimed "that the name 'hero' (*hērōs*) is only a slightly altered form of the word 'love' (*erōs*)–the very thing from which the heroes sprang."[5] Plato says a second reason they may have been called heroes was because they were clever speech-makers (*rhētores*) and were also skilled in dialectical questioning (*erōtan*). The development of these linguistic powers is the key for Vico to heroic mind as the ultimate ideal of human education. Heroic mind is to be sought in all subjects. In the last oration of his career delivered to the Academy of Oziosi (1737), not as one of his university orations, Vico continues his theme of the importance of eloquence. He reaffirms the power of eloquence in human affairs citing among other examples Cicero's speech in defense of Quintus Ligarius before Caesar at the Council. As Caesar, ruler of the known world, left the proceedings he declared "Had Cicero not spoken so well today, Ligarius would not flee from our hands."[6] The power of the law depends upon the power of rhetoric. Rhetoric is not only the key to prudence; it is the key to jurisprudence.

Throughout his career Vico taught from his own textbook of institutes, *Institutiones oratoriae* (1711–41). The legal principles conveyed were interpretations of Roman law, the *Corpus iuris civilis*. In the class session Vico dictated a portion of the textbook in Latin to the students during the first half hour. In the second half hour the dictated material was expanded upon and explained, all in Latin. The basis of legal education in civil law required a mastery of Latin, the principles of rhetorical speech, and the application of these to Roman law. The center of legal education was to prepare students to speak in the law courts backed by a sound knowledge of jurisprudence.

Vico himself was an autodidact in all the fields of human studies including the law. Having withdrawn from the Jesuit school in which he was enrolled in his early years, Vico briefly, but without registering for them, attended some university lectures on cannon law by Felice Aquadies and remained for two months in a privately given law course of Francesco Verde

---

4. Vico, *Study Methods*, xxii.
5. Plato, *Cratylus*, 398d.
6. Vico, *Study Methods*, 85–90.

before dropping out, being dissatisfied with their minute detail. He continued his study of cannon and civil law on his own and under the tutelage of the attorney Fabrizio del Vecchio, Vico developed a grasp of practical forensics. His one experience in court was three days before his eighteenth birthday in 1686. Having petitioned for admission to the Bar, Vico obtained permission to and successfully defended his father (a bookseller) in a civil action brought against him by a rival bookseller Bartolomeo Moreschi.[7] Shortly after his success in this case Vico accepted a position as tutor to the children of the Rocca family traveling with them to their castle at Vatolla, a three-day carriage ride south of Naples in the mountains of the Cilento. While at Vatolla Vico read through the library of the Fransiscan convent of Santa Maria della Pietà, thus completing his general education in humane letters as well as metaphysics. During the nine years he held this position, Vico returned on occasion with the Rocca family to Naples. Although not in regular residence at Naples Vico matriculated at the University and received a doctorate in both laws, canon and civil.

Vico's sense of eloquence extends from the practice of the law to the practice of teaching. To speak in the law courts is to orate. To speak in the classroom is also to orate. Eloquence requires one to speak fully on a subject, to present all of its aspects in a complete speech conveying to the hearers all that the speaker has conceived in his mind. At the end of his autobiography Vico says that in his teaching he attempted to practice the ideal of the great tradition of the Humanists: to be "wisdom speaking." Vico paraphrases this Ciceronian view in the conclusion to his seventh oration.[8] Eloquence requires *copia* as it brings together many aspects of a subject, but it differs from elegance in that eloquent speech is a presentation of the whole, whereas elegant speech refers to the fineness of the phraseology used.

Vico says in his autobiography that he not only attempted to be wisdom speaking, he further lectured "as if famous men of letters had come from abroad to attend his classes and to hear him."[9] There is, in fact, no other ideal that a true teacher can have. Anything less is not appropriate to learned speech. Vico says that he was always afraid of being alone in wisdom for such solitude makes one either a god or a fool, and he says, "Though I am afraid of delivering false judgments an all subjects, I am par-

---

7. Vico, *Autobiography*, 117.
8. Vico, *Study Methods*, 78.
9. Vico, *Autobiography*, 199.

ticularly afraid of advancing erroneous views on eloquence, since I profess it."[10] The antidote to being alone is wisdom, which is the risk of every original thinker, is eloquence. Eloquence allows the thinker to communicate his discoveries to an audience, to present wisdom in its proper form and to avoid simply the juggling of words.

Behind Vico as professor of Latin eloquence is Vico as *grammaticus*. Vico's eloquence is based on his practice of the art of the ancient grammarians, the attempt to ground one's thought and speech in the true meanings of words as is pursued in Plato's *Cratylus* and in Varro's *De lingua latina*. In his attack on Descartes' metaphysics in *The Most Ancient Wisdom of the Italians Unearthed from the Origins of the Latin Language* Vico claims that the intellectual meanings of words in ancient Latin came into it from the pre-Socratic philosophers of Ionia who were experts in reasoning about the physical world and from the Etruscans who were experts in divine ideas.[11] Such intellectual meanings could not be original to the speakers of old Latin as it was primarily a language of farmers and soldiers. Vico also follows this procedure of tracing words back to their origin in his *Universal Law* and in his *New Science*. He repeatedly shows that the key terms of Roman law have etymologies that reveal the meanings of the customs out of which Roman and human society itself is generated. For example he traces the claim to right of ownership, the *vindiciae*, found originally as a legal principle in the *Law of the Twelve Tables* back to the custom of duels as the original means for the settling of disputes between two parties.[12]

Vico's *Universal Law* is the first version of what was to become his *New Science of the Common Nature of the Nations* (1725 and 1730/1744), the central concept of which is derived from the Roman *ius gentium* which Vico formulates as *ius gentium naturale* or "the natural law of the peoples." In essence *ius gentium* asserts that there is a part of the *ius civile* or private law of any nation that is held in common with every other nation. Vico transposes this legal principle into his historical principle of *storia ideale eterna*, "ideal eternal history." He does this by a *nuova arte critica*, "new critical art" in which philosophy with its formulation of universal principles is applied to philology with its concentration on the particulars of the human world. The grammatical pursuit of the original meanings of words is expanded into philology defined by Vico as the study of all things that "depend on human

10. Vico, *Study Methods*, 80.
11. Vico, *Ancient Wisdom*, 37–40.
12. Vico, *New Science*, par. 961.

choice; for example, all histories of the languages, customs, and deeds of peoples in war and peace."[13] Vico's ideal eternal history conceives all nations as developing through the same general pattern of an age of gods in which all of nature and all basic social institutions are comprehended as the presence of gods, an age of heroes, in which the virtues necessary to archaic societies are embodied in the characters and deeds of heroes, and the age of men, in which social life is governed by written law and abstract forms of thought. Vico in his conception of "ideal eternal history" temporalizes the principle of the commonality of nations present in a static sense in the conception of *ius gentium* of Roman law. Underlying this common course of all nations is Vico's version of the *sensus communis*.

Sensus Communis

As a philosophical, rhetorical, and literary term, *sensus comuunis* can be understood in four main senses. It is understood in two ways by the ancients and in two ways by the moderns.

(1) In Aristotelian psychology, *aisthesis koine* (common sense, *sensus communis*) is a faculty of the *psyche* that perceives those aspects of the external world that are not the province of one of the particular five senses. That which is not the result of the specific function of any one of the five senses are "common sensibles." Aristotle says: "Common sensibles are movement, rest, number, figure, magnitude; these are not special to any one sense, but are common to all."[14] He says that there cannot be a special sense-organ for the common sensible: "it is clearly impossible for there to be a special sense of any one of these common sensibles, e.g. movement; for, if there were, we should perceive them in the same way as we now perceive what is sweet by sight."[15] The fact that we perceive a thing by our sense of sight and also perceive it as sweet by our sense of taste is incidental to the thing, to its particular qualities. The common sensibles are properties of all perceivable things. Our five senses present us with the particular properties of particular things. Aristotle's distinction between common sensibles and the special five senses is similar to the later distinction in Galilean science between primary and secondary qualities. The primary qualities are those features of things that are mathematically measurable; the secondary quali-

---

13. Vico, *New Science*, par. 7.
14. Aristotle, *De anima*, 418a.
15. Ibid., 425a.

ties are subjective, dependent on and variable with the observer. But for Aristotle both the common and the particular properties of the object are derived from the power of perception and are there as such in the object.

(2) Although *sensus communis* is the corresponding Latin term for *aisthesis koine*, the Roman Stoics developed a very different sense of it. For the Stoics "common sense" is a rhetorical and social term. In the Aristotelian sense it is a psychological and epistemological term. Seneca in his *Epistle* "On Facing the World with Confidence" advises that hatred (*odium*) can be avoided in human affairs by never provoking anyone. But if one encounters hatred from others when it is uncalled for by one's actions toward them "common sense will keep you safe from it [*a qou te sensus communis tuebitur*]."[16] Common sense in this context has the sense of acting moderately and well toward others in the manner of a good and decent person. One presents oneself as someone to be respected, as someone not to be feared or hated or as a danger to others. This Stoic sense of self-possession is the basis of confidence in facing the ways of the world. Seneca's *sensus communis* as a guide to human conduct is a Stoic version of the cardinal virtue of temperance (*temperantia*) of which Cicero says: "Under this head is further included what in Latin may be called *decorum* (propriety); for in Greek it is called *prepon*. Such is its essential nature, that it is inseparable from moral goodness; for what is proper is morally right, and what is morally right is proper."[17] Cicero says further that *decorum* or propriety is so much a part of all virtues "that it is perfectly self-evident and does not require any abstruse process of reasoning to see it."[18] To learn propriety we must observe how for the poets "every action is in accord with each individual character."[19] Cicero's *decorum* or propriety is a doctrine of prudence in human affairs but is accompanied by eloquence in speech and thought.

Juvenal, in satirizing the pompous use of social class and pedigrees in civil affairs, says of persons who hold by these, "It's pretty rare that you'll find considerateness in people of that class [*rarus enim ferme sensus communis in illa fortuna*]."[20] *Sensus communis* here is a principle of thoughtful kindness derived from an awareness of the commonality all have with each other as human beings as opposed to feelings of pomposity and superior-

16. Seneca, *Epistles*, 105.4.
17. Cicero, *De officiis*, 1.27.93–94.
18. Ibid., 1.27.95.
19. Ibid., 1.28.97.
20. Juvenal, *Satires*, 8.73–74.

ity. Horace in characterizing various kinds of faults committed in human relationships speaks of someone being "quite devoid of social tact [*communi sensu plane caret inquimus*]."[21] Seneca in his essay "On Benefits" says, "Social tact should be used in bestowing a benefit [*Sit in beneficio sensus communis*]."[22] To have *sensus communis* is to know how to act with propriety in any social situation, to do what is fitting with particular conditions in bestowing a benefit and not to interfere with the concerns or occupations of another.

Marcus Aurelius, in formulating his Stoic philosophy in his *Meditations*, coins a Greek term that Shaftesbury finds closely associated with a wider sense of *sensus communis* and on which Gadamer comments in his discussion of the humanist tradition in *Truth and Method*.[23] This very attractive term is *koinonoemosune*.[24] It has the sense of "public spirit," of "common sensibility," what is shared, public, and common to all people. This term, if associated with *sensus communis*, takes us beyond social tact to the idea of a shared sensibility upon which society and civility depend. It is more than a sentiment necessary for successful relationships between individuals; it is the sentiment necessary for society itself to function.

(3) Among the Moderns, Descartes employs a concept of common sense that differs from that of both Aristotle and the Stoics. In the first line of his *Discourse on the Method* (1637) Descartes claims, "Good sense [*le bon sens*] is the best distributed thing in the world: for everyone thinks himself so well endowed with it that even those who are the hardest to please in everything else do not usually desire more of it than they possess."[25] Descartes' "*le bon sens*" is the rational ability to recognize what comes before the mind as a clear and distinct idea; it is required in order to recognize first principles from which right reasoning can proceed according to his method. *Le bon sens* is not an inductive power to reason from or hold sound opinions based on empirical experience. It is not a way of thinking in rhetorical terms, that is, in a verisimilar, probable, or dialectical manner.

In the eighteenth century common-sense philosophy is developed primarily by French and Scottish thinkers. Descartes' answer to skepticism is taken up in a new way by Claude Buffier (1661–1737). For Buffier in

---

21. Ibid., 1.3.66.
22. Seneca, *Moral Essays*, 1.11.3.
23. Gadamer, *Truth and Method*, pt. 1.
24. Marcus Aurelius, *Meditations*, 1.16.2.
25. Descartes, *Discourse*, 1:111.

his work of *First Truths* (trans. 1780) common sense is an unimpeachable authority that allows us to process such first truths as the existence of the external world, that mind is incorporeal, and that there is free will. For Buffier such truths have been acknowledged by the majority of humanity. Any who skeptically reject such truths, still find themselves in their life acting in accord with them.

Thomas Reid's *An Inquiry into the Human Mind on the Principles of Common Sense* (1764) founds the Scottish Common Sense School. Reid thought the truths of common sense to be evident in ordinary language. Reid claimed that although such truths cannot be made evident by deductive proof, when philosophers attempt to reason against them, their language fails to make good sense. For Descartes common sense as "good sense" lets us recognize rational first truths when we encounter them. For Reid common sense acts as a corrective when we pursue reason to the point of holding incoherent views. Descartes and Reid in their different ways anticipate the generally modern view that common sense is an epistemic power, a way of knowing what is proto-scientific. This proto-scientific sense is captured in the German expression for common sense— *gesunder Menschenverstand*, "sound or healthy human understanding." As *gesunder Menschenverstand* our common sense view of the world is a more loosely organized form of knowledge than that of science. Scientific reasoning, on this view, takes common sense understanding as a beginning point and develops a more precise account of the world through observation, experiment, and theoretical formulations.

(4) At odds with the distinctively modern view of common sense, whether that found in Descartes' rationalism or Reid's empiricism, is Shaftesbury's view in the second treatise of his *Characteristiks*: "Sensus Communis; An Essay on the Freedom of Wit and Humour" (1709). Shaftesbury wishes to revive the social and moral sense of *sensus communis* found among the Latin writers and the Stoics. Shaftesbury portrays a conversation among friends concerning morality and religion and raises the question of how differences of opinion could be resolved in these matters. It is suggested that such differences could be settled by an appeal to common sense, which leads one participant to the question of what common sense is. But differences in religion and morality appear to be present in any attempt to say what constitutes common sense. Shaftesbury says: "If by the word *Sense* we were to understand Opinion and Judgment, and by the word *common* the Generality or any considerable part of mankind; 'twou'd be hard, he

said, to discover where the Subject of common Sense cou'd lie. For that which was according to the Sense of one part of Mankind, was against the Sense of another."[26]

Shaftesbury draws on the Latin poets and on the Stoics to revive a view of the moral or social sense of common sense. As mentioned above, he is particularly impressed with the coining of *koinonoemosune* by Marcus Aurelius—the sense of "public spirit." Shaftesbury advocates the "*Sense* of *Publik Weal*, and of the *Common Interest*; Love of the *Community* or *Society*, natural Affection, Humanity, Obligingness, or that sort of *Civility* which rises from a just *Sense* of the *common Rights* of Mankind, and the *natural Equality* there is among those of the same Species."[27] Shaftesbury understands common sense as a universal sentiment upon which civil society itself depends and thus a sentiment that cuts across the diversity of religions, moralities, and societies. He says, "A publick Spirit can come only from a social Feeling or *Sense of Partnership* with human Kind."[28] Shaftesbury intends his common sense to be the original sentiment from which human society itself arises and to stand in opposition to the natural-law theory of a "state of nature." We arrive at this principle of public spiritedness or common fellowship after realizing that no principle of commonality can be advanced through the abstractions of philosophical reasoning. Shaftesbury's principle of common sense is close to Hume's principle of "common life" of the third book of *A Treatise of Human Nature*.[29] For Hume the unsuccessful pursuit of an accord among philosophical doctrines that leads to skepticism leads on to the realization of the importance of common life that underlies all civility and makes the human world possible.

Vico's conception of *sensus communis* contains elements of all four conceptions delineated above. The twelfth axiom of Vico's *New Science* defines his conception: "Common sense [*il senso comune*] is judgment without reflection, shared by an entire class, an entire people, an entire nation, or the entire human race."[30] This definition extends and clarifies Vico's remarks on *sensus communis* in the third section of his seventh oration.[31] Vico's *senso comune* does not embody Aristotle's conception of a faculty of

26. Shaftesbury, *Characteristicks*, 50.
27. Ibid., 66.
28. Ibid., 67.
29. Hume, *Treatise*, 455.
30. Vico, *New Science*, par.142.
31. Vico, *Study Methods*, 13.

common sense but it is in accord with Aristotle in understanding common sense to derive from sensation. As will be discussed in the next section on topics, Vico's conception of common sense is grounded in his conception of "sensory topics." Vico incorporates the Latin conception of common sense as "social tact" into his view that common sense can be something shared by a class, a people, or a nation. Thus common sense can vary from class to class, people to people, or nation to nation, but every such social order requires its version of it to attain its own particular identity. Descartes' "*bon sens*" and Reid's "common sense" understood as epistemic conceptions of *sensus communis*, are involved in Vico's definition in the phrase "judgment without reflection." But for Vico common sense is a standard and means for forming judgments, a kind of knowledge but one that is not based on reflection as scientific or theoretical judgments are.

Shaftesbury's principle of common sense is perhaps closest to Vico's in that Vico's common sense is "communal sense" that can extend to "the entire human race." In Italian a municipality was originally called and is still called a *comune*. Shaftesbury limits his conception of the commonality inherent in *sensus communis* to ethical or social terms. Vico's *senso comune* is ethical and social but it is also metaphysical. Vico further explains his sense of common in his thirteenth axiom: "Uniform ideas originating among entire peoples unknown to each other must have a common ground of truth [*un motivo comune di vero*]."[32] This axiom reflects the sense of "common" in Vico's full title of his *New Science—Principles of New Science Concerning the Common [Comune] Nature of the Nations*. What is common to the nations is the "natural law of the gentes [*il diritto natural delle genti*]" which Vico bases on the Roman *ius gentium* as discussed above. From the common nature of the nations there "issues the mental dictionary [*il dizionario mentale*] for assigning origins to all the diverse articulated languages. It is by means of this dictionary that the ideal eternal history is conceived which gives us the history in time of all nations."[33] The understanding of this dictionary takes us back to the connection between eloquence and *sensus communis* that Vico claims in the seventh oration, the key to which is Vico's insistence on the importance of *ars topica* for both human education and human knowledge. The mental dictionary is tied to law and legal education as it is the ultimate source from which meanings can be drawn to plead a case or interpret the law in a legal proceeding.

32. Vico, *New Science*, par. 144.
33. Ibid., par. 145.

Moral Philosophy and Moral Education

Ars Topica, Ars Memoria

The art of topics makes minds inventive in the art of reasoning. The art of criticism makes them exact. The art of topics cannot be separated from the art of memory. The two greatest Latin writers on rhetoric, Cicero and Quintilian, relate the following concerning the interconnection of memory and places (*topoi, loci*).

The poet Simonides of Ceos, who is said to be the first to charge for the composition of poetry, was commissioned by a prosperous nobleman called Scopas to present an epinicion for a victorious boxer at a banquet for which he was the host. Simonides chanted his poem to the banqueters which included a substantial digression singing the praises of the beloved brothers, Castor and Pollux. His digression was not wholly inappropriate as Pollux or Polydeuces was famous as a boxer. Scopas, displeased by the digression, meanly withheld half of Simonides' fee saying that he could seek the other half from these sons of Tyndareus (king of Sparta) since he had devoted an equal share of his poem to praising them, taking attention away from the praise due him as host.

During the banquet a message was brought to Simonides saying that there were two young men outside the hall who urgently demanded to speak with him. Simonides exited the hall to respond to their call but found no one. Just as he crossed the threshold, the hall collapsed crushing to death Scopas and all the guests. They were so badly crushed that when their relatives came the next day to bury them they were unable to tell the bodies apart for individual burial. Simonides, however, was able to assist the relatives by recalling the place where each had reclined at the table. This procedure prompted his discovery of the connection between places and memory, making him the founder of mnemonics. He had indeed been rewarded by Castor and Pollux.[34]

Simonides' discovery of the connection between places and memory resulted in the technique of "artificial memory."[35] This technique is not artificial in the sense of something false but in the sense of an artifice, something made. The orator in preparing a speech impresses on his mind the scenes or images of a series of places, for example rooms in a private villa or public building. Moving from room to room he associates the first

---

34. Cicero, *De Oratore*, 2.86.351–53; Quintilian, *Institutio oratoria*, 11. 2.11–16. See the retelling of this tale by Yates, *Art of Memory*, 1–2.

35. Yates, *Art of Memory*, chap. 1.

major point of his speech with the first room, the second with the second room, and so forth. It is desirable that the rooms or places employed have different characters, shapes, or furnishings so that they form distinct impressions on the imagination. To deliver the speech the orator recalls each of the rooms or places in order. The recall of each reminds him of the next point he wishes to make in his speech. This technique of artificial memory provides the orator with an inner writing, an invisible text present in his memory from which he can call forth each of his themes and sub-themes and expand upon them in an apparently extemporaneous manner. The key to his eloquence is his pre-established system of *topoi* or *loci* which guide every step of his treatment of his subject. These places once well committed to memory can be used and reused as a master series of images upon which the points of other speeches are placed and delivered.

In contrast to this ancient technique of the artificial memory which applies to standard forms of oratory is the Renaissance conception of the "theatre of memory." The greatest example of this is put forth by Guilio Camillo in his little treatise *L'idea del theatro* (1550). The theatre of memory is a part of the larger tradition of the *theatrum mundi*, "the theatre of the world," the theatre as microcosm of the world and the world, especially the human world, as theatre in which each person plays a role.[36] The theatre of memory is closely associated with Vico's common mental dictionary as will be explained shortly. Camillo's theatre, which was actually constructed in France and in Italy, is a metaphysics based on a system of memory-places connected to the rhetorical principles of oratory. The spectator or practitioner of the system of the theatre entered on the stage facing an audience of images or *pitture* depicting figures and elements of Greco-Roman and Judeo-Christian mythology arranged as seven grades intersected by seven gangways.

These are the master images from which the human world has made or drawn forth itself. They are joined with a system of places whereby the spectator may commit or recommit them to memory. The technique required is like that of artificial memory except unlike the places of artificial memory these places are not arbitrary. They are the formations natural to the human mind itself, understood as reflection of the divine *mens*. They are archetypes from which the human world arises and to which it constantly returns in all of its activity. In the theatre were coffers or drawers containing manuscripts of Cicero and other ancients suggesting that the

---

36. Ibid., chap. 6. See also Bernheimer, "Theatrum mundi," 225–47.

goal of the spectator, once he passively mastered the retention in memory of the *pitture*, could actively compose the complete speech of humanity. This speech would result in a rhetorically-based metaphysics.

In similarity with any metaphysics this speech would purport to be complete in principle but would not include every detail of experience. It would be logical in the sense that, as Aristotle claims in the first sentence of his *Rhetoric*,[37] rhetoric is a counterpart of dialectic. It would not be a metaphysics logically deduced from self-evident first principles. In this sense it would be a metaphysics opposite in its conception to that advocated by Descartes. The "first principles" of the metaphysics of memory are the commonplaces of humanity. Yet from these commonplaces can be drawn a total account of the interconnections of the natural, civil, and divine worlds since these interconnections are what are formed within the forces and structures of each of the master images of the theatre. Ultimately the theatre is the fulfillment of the aim of self-knowledge of Socratic philosophy, for in it the individual is offered a device to confront his own nature writ large. All that we are as human beings lies in memory. What we require is a means to recall it. Camillo's theatre purports to provide us with the places necessary for the ultimate eloquence, to be "wisdom speaking," putting the whole of things into words by drawing the whole of human wisdom forth from its origins, its original expressions in the myths.

Ars topica in artificial memory is based on places that exist for other purposes than their use in producing an inner writing for oration. In the *ars topica* of the theatre of memory the system of places is the result of the system of images they govern. Both of these types of memory employ topics as physical places. The art of topics presented by Aristotle in his logical treatise on *Topics* and in his *Rhetoric* and by Cicero in his short text *Topica* do not involve topics as physical places. Topics in this sense are mental places or common places that are universal forms or types of propositions from which specific lines of argumentation can be invented depending upon what sort of issue or question has been raised. There are general forms of argument employed in probable reasoning as distinguished from demonstrative or deductive reasoning that proceeds from self-evident principles. *Topos* is akin to Greek *topazein* "to aim at or guess."

This sense of topics is at the basis of forensic or juridical oratory. Given the specific cause raised, the forensic orator can go in his mind to one or more of the universal forms of argumentation that applies and

37. Aristotle, *Rhetoric*, 854a1.

find a guideline to the specific argument required to defend or prosecute a case. As Aristotle says in the first sentence of the *Topics* the purpose of the study of topics is "to discover a method by which we shall be able to reason from generally accepted opinions about any problem set before us and shall ourselves, when sustaining an argument, avoid saying anything self-contradictory."[38] Cicero says, "It is easy to find things that are hidden if the hiding place is pointed out and marked; similarly if we wish to track down some argument we ought to know the places or topics: for that is the name given by Aristotle to the 'regions' [*sedes*], as it were, from which arguments are drawn."[39] The list of topics found in Aristotle and Cicero differ. Cicero, although he refers to Aristotle, may not have been working from Aristotle's actual text. Cicero presents his list of topics in a way that is closest to that of Vico in his above-mentioned textbook on rhetoric. This may be because Cicero's list is specifically developed in relation to legal reasoning using examples from Roman law.

Cicero discusses "definition, partition, etymology, conjugates, genus, species, similarity, difference, contraries, adjuncts, consequents, antecedents, contradictions, causes, effects, and comparisons of things greater, less and equal."[40] He says that in inverting an argument more than one of these topics may be required but the use of all of them in constructing a single argument is never likely to occur. It is not my purpose to summarize what each of these topics is but it is not difficult to comprehend how they work. If we are faced with an argument or case that depends upon a certain definition, then it is important to know in advance the general principles or rules of definition and employ them to confront the specific issue. The same can be said of knowing in advance of a specific issue what an argument from antecedent or consequent is or in regard to causes the difference between a remote and a proximate cause or the nature of contrariety versus contradiction, and so forth. By knowing the topics in this sense one knows in advance all the possible forms an argument can take regardless of the specific subject. Once the relevant universal form is found a mental place is present from which to produce a specific line of reasoning pro and con.

Aristotle at the close of his *Topics* draws a parallel between topics as categories in which arguments fall and places from which things can be remembered. He says: "in arguments [as in geometry and arithmetic] it is

---

38. Aristotle, *Topics*, 100a18–21.
39. Cicero, *Topica*, 2.7–8.
40. Ibid., 18.71.

Moral Philosophy and Moral Education

important to be prompt about first principles and to know your premisses by heart. For just as to a trained memory the mere reference to the places in which they occur causes the things themselves to be remembered, so the above rules will make a man a better reasoner, because he sees the premisses defined and numbered. A premiss of general application should be committed to memory rather than an argument. . . ."[41] By "premiss" here Aristotle means that which is first, the general form or presupposition on which the argument in question is based. As with the artificial memory the places studied in advance guide the oration so with forensic oration or reasoning the topics studied in advance guide the argumentation.

In the seventh oration Vico extends the *ars topica* to the art of securing the middle term (*terminus medius*). The middle term is that upon which eloquence depends in forensic speech. Vico says: "Traditional 'topics' is the art of finding 'the *medium*,' i.e., the middle term: in the conventional language of Scholasticism, 'medium' indicates what the Latins call *argumentum*. Those who know all the *loci*, i.e., the lines of argument to be used, are able (by an operation not unlike reading the characters on a page) to group extemporaneously the elements of persuasion in any question or case."[42] The middle term is that which appears in both the major and the minor of the syllogism. By connecting each of the two terms of the conclusion to the same middle term, the syllogism claims their connection as the subject and predicate terms in the conclusion. The middle term, it is clear, makes possible the syllogism. Without the middle term, the propositions of the conclusion can be stated, but there is no argument for it. In the *Prior Analytics* Aristotle says: "For in general we stated that no deduction can establish the attribution of one thing to another, unless some middle term is taken, which is somehow related to each by way of predication."[43] In inventing a syllogism by applying the rules of the topics to a particular case, the middle term must be sought out and from it the two extremes that become the terms connected in the conclusion must, so to speak, be drawn forth from it.

In the *Posterior Analytics* Aristotle says, "Now, that everything we seek is a search for a middle term is clear."[44] The connection of the subject and predicate terms of the conclusion is that of which the speaker tries to

---

41. Aristotle, *Topics*, 163b.
42. Vico, *Study Methods*, 15.
43. Aristotle, *Prior Analytics*, 41a3.
44. Aristotle, *Posterior Analytics*, 90a35.

persuade his audience. To do this he must find a commonplace that his audience shares with him. This *topos* is the middle term. If his audience accepts the meaning of the middle term, then he must show that the other two terms are implied within it, that they can be drawn forth from it, that they are naturally part of its meaning. The more common or fundamental a commonplace is, the more successful the argument. This may require the speaker not simply to advance one single syllogism but regressively to construct a sorites or series of incomplete but interlocking syllogisms that leads back to a middle term that captures a meaning that the audience adheres to simply as part of their understanding of themselves, as part of what they share as "an entire class, an entire people, an entire nation, or the entire human race," to use Vico's words quoted above that describe his conception of common or communal sense.

In the *New Science* Vico offers a prime example of such a topic, in fact, it is the *topos* of *topoi*. He says that the minds of the first men "began to hew out topics, which is an art of regulating well the primary operation of our mind by noting the commonplaces that must be run over in order to know all there is in a thing that one desires to know well; that is, completely."[45] Thus as Vico describes them commonplaces are at the basis of eloquence for eloquence is to capture in speech the whole of a subject. These original topics or commonplaces are the first thoughts. Vico says: "The first founders of humanity applied themselves to a sensory topics, by which they brought together those properties or qualities or relations of individuals and species which were, so to speak, concrete, and from these created their poetic genera."[46] Poetic genera are what Vico elsewhere calls "imaginative universals" or "poetic characters."[47] From the experience of thunder the first men formed the thunderous sky as Jove. Jove was a "sensory *topos*." The sky becomes a place separate from earth and a god separate from men, from themselves. Vico's conception of sensory topics is dependent on his new science of the common nature of the nations. It is not to be found in standard rhetorical theory.

Sensory topics are at the basis of Vico's conception of a common mental dictionary. This mental dictionary contains all the middle terms out of which the human world is generated. It is analogous to Camillo's theatre of memory for in it are all the poetic genera that stand behind the words

45. Vico, *New Science*, par. 497.
46. Ibid., par. 495.
47. Ibid., pars. 204–10.

of all natural languages. The mental dictionary is not itself written down but all languages are particular attempts explicitly to express the meanings therein. This etymologicon is connected to Vico's discovery of the science of blazonry. Vico regards the first language to be a language of mute signs coupled with a law of force used by the first families to maintain themselves. These mute meanings were later recorded on coats of arms, military insignias, heraldry and finally appear on coins and medals. This law of force was based on the power of the fathers of the first families to take the auspices of Jove and govern by their perceptions of divine law.

The art of topics is the art whereby meaning was first established in the world. Dialectical reasoning requires the finding of persuasive arguments. Persuasion in argumentation is based on finding the appropriate middle term. The middle term is found through an art of memory that allows us to recall the commonalities out of which the mind of the audience itself has arisen. These commonalities presuppose the common mental dictionary that underlies all natural language. The orator needs to know not only topics in the sense of the universal forms of argumentation, that is, definition, partition, and so forth, but topics in the sense of the memory-places out of which the civil world itself is formed. To speak in the law courts and convince a judge and jury requires that the speaker has command of a whole education so that he can take his hearers if needed back to meanings they all share in the back of their minds and bring his specific arguments forward from these meanings, from the mental dictionary of humanity.

The Ideal Orator as Educator

The orator is, so to speak, the "middle term" that provides for the connection between the audience and the subject or cause at issue. The agenda of Western philosophy has been to attribute the origin of rhetoric to the Sophists and to separate rhetoric from the pursuit of truth claiming it to be no more than an art of words, an activity of persuasion, and in so doing an appeal to the emotions. The tale taught to all students in introductory philosophy is that the Sophists were experts were experts in making the worse appear the better case and that they even sought payment to teach others their techniques of doing this. Socrates appears as the counter to the Sophists advocating the pure pursuit of truth wherever his dialectical questioning leads regardless of its effect on his hearers. Furthermore, Socrates charges his hearers and interlocutors no fee for any instruction they may require. The principal document of this battleground is Plato's *Gorgias* in which the Platonic-Socrates confronts the venerable Gorgias famed throughout Greece for his powers of ingenuity and eloquence and his supporter Polus the author of an important treatise on rhetoric. The issue is who can know what is just and who can teach it to others, the philosopher or the rhetorician.[48]

The issue of the teachability of virtue is raised further in the *Protagoras*. Protagoras, the great sophist, with two other famous sophists in attendance, Hippias and Prodicus, claims before Socrates that he can teach young men how to deliberate and how to become good members of society. He claims that, as a sophist, an expert in the use of words, he can impart the wisdom that is necessary for the art of life in the *polis*. The dialogue remains inconclusive with Socrates uncharacteristically denying that virtue is teachable and Protagoras denying that virtue is wisdom because various virtues, especially courage, are not based on a kind of rational expertise.

In both of these dialogues the character of the sophist and rhetoric is presented in a much more complicated way than that the sophist is simply an unscrupulous teacher that makes the worse appear the better case and that rhetoric is in itself defective or bad. What Socrates shows is that the sophist like the poet as presented in *Republic* X cannot offer a coherent account of what virtue is. The sophist cannot give a coherent speech that justifies the aim of the principles of speech that he teaches, just as the poets portray the gods or men as performing virtuous actions at one time and acting badly and without virtue another. The issue of the sophist charging for his teaching is also not a telling difference with Socrates. Socrates does not need to charge for his conversations as he is informally but comfortably supported by the charity of his prominent followers such as the businessman Crito and the aristocrat Plato.

A close look at the relevant dialogues of Plato shows that the philosopher requires the use of words and the ability to persuade as does the sophist or rhetorician. Philosophy is done through words. It can only occur as a kind of dialectical oration. We see this in the *Phaedrus* in which Socrates claims that the Athenian statesman "Pericles is the most perfect orator in existence."[49] The issue of the relation of ethics to rhetoric involves the question of the *ethos* (moral character) of the speaker that is raised in Aristotle's *Rhetoric* and pursued in Cicero's *The Orator*, and Quintilian's

---

48. Plato, *Gorgias*, 461b–c.
49. Plato, *Phaedrus*, 269e.

Institutes which will be discussed below. In the *Phaedrus* Socrates speaks of the sense in which to philosopher's search for truth is intertwined with the rhetorical mastery of words. Truth can only be joined to persuasion through the art of speaking.[50] Socrates says that we must persuade young Phaedrus "that unless he pay proper attention to philosophy he will never be able to speak properly about anything" and Socrates continues "Is not rhetoric in its entire nature an art which leads the soul by means of words, not only in law courts and the various other public assemblages, but in private companies as well?"[51]

Rhetoric, Socrates claims, requires a knowledge of the soul (*psychē*). He says: "Since it is the function of speech to lead souls by persuasion, he who is to be a rhetorician must know the various forms of soul."[52] Socrates says that it is generally held that the rhetorician need not be concerned with what is true, just, and good: "For in the courts, they say, nobody comes for truth about these matters, but for that which is convincing; and that is probability, so that he who is to be an artist in speech must fix attention upon probability."[53] Socrates is not an enemy of probable speech for the *elenchos*, the method of the question and answer that he practices, is dialectic in the sense of reasoning from common opinions on a subject to seek the truth.

We do not find Socrates establishing a point by deductive reasoning from self-evident principles as aspired to by the Scholastics or Cartesian rationalism. Dialectic educates and perfects the soul by directing it toward what is ultimate; it forms the *ethos* of the speaker. Socrates thus holds with Aristotle the claim that dialectic must be joined with rhetoric. Socrates says it is a noble activity to tell stories about justice and associated ethical subjects but "serious discourse about them is far nobler, when one employs the dialectic method and plants and sows in a fitting soul intelligent words which are able to help themselves and him who planted them, which are not fruitless, but yield seed from which there spring up in other minds other words capable of continuing the process for ever, and which make their possessor happy, to the farthest possible limit of human happiness [*eudaimonia*]."[54]

---

50. Ibid., 260d.
51. Ibid., 261a–b.
52. Ibid., 271d.
53. Ibid., 272e.
54. Ibid., 276e–277a.

Rhetoric and Human Education

From these views Socrates puts forth, it does not emerge that philosophy requires the abandonment of the art of rhetoric that the sophist teaches but that rhetoric requires philosophy in order to ground the eloquent use of words and their power to persuade. And in reverse the philosopher must himself be eloquent. The Socrates of the Latins, who are much closer in time to him than we are, is a master of eloquence, not an enemy of it. Cicero in *The Orator* asks, "What is Critias? and Alcibiades? these though not benefactors of their fellow-citizens were undoubtedly learned and eloquent; and did they not owe their training to the discussions of Socrates?"[55] Cicero says that it was the verdict of all of Greece that Socrates came out on top in any debate not only because of his wisdom and subtlety but also due "to his eloquence."[56]

Quintilian says that Socrates in his dispute with Gorgias silences him with the claim that the "rhetorical man must but just, and the just man must wish to do just things."[57] Quintilian adds that it is made "even clearer in the *Phaedrus* that this art cannot be perfect without a knowledge of justice."[58] He says he agrees with this and that his answer to the view that oratory in the courts is concerned only with what is probable or a semblance of truth, not the truth itself, is that those who hold this claim must make their own justification. Quintilian concludes: "What I have undertaken is to fashion the perfect orator, and my first requirement is that he should be a good man [*esse virum bonum*]."[59]

Quintilian's insistence on the perfect orator being a good man echoes Aristotle's above-mentioned claims concerning the importance of *ethos* in oratory. This moral character is the key to Aristotle's conception of a first kind of proof in a speech. "the orator persuades by moral character when his speech is delivered in such a manner as to render him worthy of confidence." And he adds: "this confidence must be due to the speech itself, not to any perceived idea of the speaker's character."[60] In the narrative of a forensic speech in which the facts are related: "One thing is to make clear our moral purpose; for as is the moral purpose, so is the character, and as is

---

55. Cicero, *De oratore*, 3.34.139.
56. Ibid., 3.16.60.
57. Quintilian, *Institutio oratoria*, 2.15.28.
58. Ibid., 2.15.29–30.
59. Ibid., 2.15.33.
60. Aristotle, *Rhetoric*, 1356a.

the end, so is the moral purpose."⁶¹ Quintilian adds to this sense of purpose that "everything within the sphere of ethics is a subject for the orator" and that "The *ethos* which I mean, and which I want to see in a speaker, will be that which is recommended primarily by goodness: not only mild and calm, but usually attractive and polite, and pleasing and delightful to the listeners."⁶² This approach is in accord with what Cicero advocates as the cardinal virtue of temperance and is connected to his doctrine of *decorum*, his doctrine of prudence, which was mentioned earlier.

Today the view is widespread that rhetoric is simply the power to use words to appeal to the emotions and thus persuade without regard to reason or truth. Forensic or judicial speech, the speech of the courtroom and of lawyers generally, is seen as sophistic. This view is characterized not so much in the ancient terms of making the worse appear the better case as in terms that the law can be whatever it can be made out to be to suit a given purpose. This sense of making the law out to be whatever one can has always been part of legal proceedings but today as the French philosopher of technological society, Jacques Ellul, and himself the author of an important work on the history of jurisprudence, claims law has become simply an instrument of social order.⁶³ Law and order means law is order but not order in a profound sense that Socrates or Vico would recognize—as the embodiment of justice and human virtue and wisdom itself.

Most of the law in modern practice would not be recognized by the Greeks or the Latins or Vico who saw the law as a system of civil wisdom to be studied to achieve the distinctively human goal of self-knowledge, that is, the key to what is meant to be a human being as a social and rational animal and as practiced to be tied to speaking in the public forum of the law courts. Instead most law is practiced behind closed doors, with great similarity to an elaborate technical procedure. In public the law is apprehended often as a matter of securing social justice as if social justice were justice. But justice is the ultimate virtue that is tied to wisdom as a knowledge of things human and divine and is that to which society must answer. Social justice is not something universal; it is a claim to a right or rights of a particular person or class of persons related to private law. Justice, like *ius*, is universal. It is the highest of the four cardinal virtues that stands as

---

61. Ibid., 1417a8.
62. Quintilian, *Institutio oratoria*, 6.2.11–13.
63. Ellul, *Technological Society*, chap. 4.

a principle above any society or condition and to which all that is human must answer to remain human.

For Vico the purpose of legal education was, as it was for the Ancients and the Italian Humanists, not only to learn the law but to learn how to speak in the law courts. Learning the law was not simply training in analyzing cases and understanding particular laws and their place in bodies of statutes; its foundation was the full study of jurisprudence as a form of human wisdom. The Cartesian method so important for grounding the new science of nature, as Vico realized, offered no guidance, no theory of knowledge for the conduct of human affairs. Cartesianism, in this sense, is uncivil. No sense of prudence or decorum can be derived from it.

Conclusion

What we have lost in the modern world is the perception behind Vico's assertion in the *New Science* that "all ancient Roman law was a serious poem, represented by the Romans in the forum, and ancient jurisprudence was a severe poem."[64] The idea that jurisprudence was *una severa poesia* is lost to us.[65] On this view, the law is apprehended as alive, as a sacred precinct to which mortals must answer. What presides over this precinct is philosophy in concert with eloquence.

Vico says, "philosophy should make the virtues understood in their idea. . . . And from the philosophies providence permitted eloquence to arise."[66] He says further: "the recovered maxims of the philosophers concerning virtue are of use only when employed by a good eloquence for kindling the feelings to do the duties of virtue."[67] Plato holds that most men are asleep; his philosophy is a call for the sleepers to awaken. Vico can say the same specifically in relation to the study and practice of jurisprudence. When an activity, form of thought, or institution becomes thin and tired the only way to revive or resurrect it is to return to its origin and attempt a palingenesis of its spirit and its original role in human education.

The law, which is available to and understandable by any person, is moral education writ large. It is the repository of civil wisdom, the wisdom that is needed for the moral education of the individual and the standard

---

64. Vico, *New Science*, 1037.
65. White, *Heracles' Bow*, esp. chaps. 5 and 6.
66. Vico, *New Science*, par. 1101.
67. Ibid., par. 1110.

to which the individual may turn for normative guidance. Jurisprudence is in largest terms the embodiment of moral philosophy. Law that is any less than this is not truly law, but just a set of rules to which the individual must answer. Moral education requires attention to the ideal of self-knowledge, which requires us as individuals to recapitulate in our own terms the stages that consciousness itself passes through in its development from its most rudimentary apprehension of the object to its most advanced self-formation of the object. The *Bildung* of this self-development of consciousness can then be connected to the education of the individual in the law. In this way, the law is understood as a source of moral wisdom that has accumulated in the development of human society itself.

7

The Aesthetic Dimension of Education

Art and Symbolic Form

Close to the art of oratory and the art of jurisprudence as guides to human conduct is the art of poetry as well as the plastic arts. Art is not rightly conceived as an instrument of morality as some aesthetic theories would hold. But art is a product of the freedom of the individual to engage in self-determination. Artistic freedom is crucial to any democratic society, which also requires rhetorical freedom or freedom of the word and the image in all their forms. How art is to be understood in relation to the moral and to theory of virtue is a problem that begins in the tenth book of the *Republic* and remains yet with us. In what follows, I wish to turn to Cassirer's conception of art as a symbolic form, as a form of human knowledge as a means to consider this problem—to access the educational value of art. In so doing, I wish to continue to take human education in the same terms in which it has been presented in the foregoing discussions.

Among the papers that Ernst Cassirer left at his death in 1945 is a fully written out lecture labeled "Seminar of Education, March 10th, 1943" which also bears the title "The Educational Value of Art."[1] The text begins with discussion of the Platonic quarrel with the poets and moves through views of various thinkers especially Croce and Collingwood. Cassirer had planned to have a volume on art included in the *Philosophy of Symbolic Forms* in addition to those on *Language, Mythical Thought*, and *The Phenomenology of Knowledge*. In these three volumes he often mentions the triad of language, myth, and art, but he says little of art as such.

As mentioned in relation to his view of history as symbolic form in Chapter 2, Cassirer in May 1942 in a letter to the American philosopher

---

1. Cassirer, *Symbol, Myth, and Culture*, 196.

and editor of the volume of critical essays on his work in *The Library of Living Philosophers* series, Paul Schilpp, wrote that he had intended to produce a volume on art but the disfavor (*Ungunst*) of the times caused him to put it off again and again.[2] The principal sources of Cassirer's aesthetics are his chapter on art in *An Essay on Man* and two lectures in addition to that on the educational value of art called "Language and Art I & II,"[3] which parallel his earlier small study, *Language and Myth*. Cassirer's conception of art as a symbolic form is derived from his conception of human culture as a systematic structure of symbolic forms that has as its main components: myth and religion, language, art, history, and science, the chapter titles of the second part of *An Essay on Man*. In addition to these forms of culture there is a "metaphysics of symbolic forms," the subject of a fourth volume of the *Philosophy of Symbolic Forms* left in manuscript at his death.

I wish to raise two questions: First, how does Cassirer conceive art as a symbolic form? And second, what are the implications of his conception for a conception of the ideals of aesthetic education? My aim in pursuing these questions is not to argue for the correctness of Cassirer's views but to attempt to establish what his views in fact are. Little has been written directly on Cassirer's conception of art relative to the frequency with which his name is mentioned in general discussions of aesthetics. Cassirer's conception of education is a nearly unexamined subject.

The Platonic Quarrel: *Mimesis*

Cassirer says, "Of all the problems that we have to study in a philosophy of education, the problem of the educational value of art is one of the most difficult ones."[4] He claims that this problem goes back to the beginning of philosophy itself and that at present we are still very far from a generally accepted solution. Plato's famous quarrel with the poets in the tenth book of the *Republic* is important not simply for an understanding of ancient aesthetics, but for philosophy's conception of itself.

The basic tenets of this quarrel are well known. I wish to review them here toward the goal of suggesting an original view of it that is derivable from Cassirer's approach. The issue is whether poetry or philosophy is the means to truth. The works of Homer had scriptural status for the Greeks

2. Ibid., 25.
3. Ibid., 145–95.
4. Ibid., 196.

and were thought to contain all that was necessary for civil wisdom. *Poiein* is to make and to compose poetry. The ancient poet is a maker of truth claims through language. The quarrel rests on the fact that the philosopher is also a maker of truth claims formulated in words. Is the relatively new figure in Plato's time of the *philosophos*, the friend or lover of wisdom, a new kind of poet, or is the philosopher a bringer of a new type of knowledge, different in kind from that of poetry? Plato's problem is to make clear the difference between Homer and Socrates.

In the *Sophist*, the productive arts (*poetikai technai*) are divided into divine and human craftsmanship and there is another kind of productivity that is shared by god and human beings.⁵ This type does not produce originals but copies (*eikōnes*). This type depends on *mimesis*, which governs the art of the poet, painter, sculptor, and actor. The craftsman (*demiourgos*) if divine produces the original. In the *Republic*, the god produces the *eidos* of the bed.⁶ The carpenter produces the physical, sensible object of the bed but it is only an *eikōn* in relation to the *eidos* of the bed. Yet this physical bed is the original for the painter whose product imitates it. The problem concerns whether the activity of the carpenter or the artist has as its product an entity that is ontologically inferior to its model (*paradeigma*). Plato thus through the principle of *mimesis* distinguishes between a true reality and a mimetic reality. The knowledge of images, *eikasia*, is the lowest segment on Plato's Divided Line. True knowledge (*episteme*) will be of originals only. Opinion (*doxa*) will be of the imitative being of sensible particulars. But that of art, of *techne poietike mimetike*, will be of shadows of the sensible second order "originals."

The ontological and epistemological distinction between *eidē* and *eikōnes* is the basis of Plato's claim to replace the poets as the traditional teachers of wisdom with the philosophers. Plato objects to the fine arts and their practitioners on two grounds: they are untrue and they are dangerous as a guide to human conduct. *Phronesis* or practical wisdom upon which proper human conduct is founded and through which civil wisdom is attained requires virtue. A virtuous act is something made in a sense analogous to the way in which a sensible object is mimetic of an *eidos*. The virtuous act must have a consistency with its model. It cannot imitate both a virtue and its opposite vice. The poets are governed by imagination that is rooted in sensation (*aisthesis*). They trust in their senses and are unable

---

5. Plato, *Sophist*, 265b.
6. Plato, *Republic*, 596b.

to discern the hidden *logos* in things. Thus they have no principle of *noesis*, no noetic grasp of the nature of things. The poets will imitate equally acts of virtue and vice; they portray both good and evil without hesitation. The poets cannot supply through their productions a standard of conduct because they have no access to the *eidē*.

Achilles is the very image of courage. But we cannot also allow him to say as Homer does that he would rather be a serf to a lesser man alive on earth than to be the king over the dead in Hades.[7] How can we learn courage from such conflicting claims? Plato says: "But as long as poetry is not able to make its apology, when we listen to it, we will chant this argument we are making to ourselves as a counter charm, taking care against falling back into this love, which is childish and belongs to the many."[8] Poetry can make no apology (defense) for itself for it lacks the *elenchos*. Philosophy is the counter charm to poetry's inborn charm to which we are always prone to return, as to that which we originally loved as the medium of our childhood imagination.

The poets ask no questions. Poetry cannot produce the *elenchos* in which the meaning of a virtue can be sought. The poet can produce an image of simply anything, which is the inherent power of the imagination. But poetry has within it no method for the judging of images. Any sensible object can be formed as an image in an indefinite number of ways, all of which are equally valid as images of it. The poet, dominated by the power of the image, has no way to know what he or she does not know. The poet has no sense of ignorance that only the device of the question and answer of the *elenchos* can command and produce in its participants. At the most basic level the poet or the rhapsode, the teller or the reteller of the myth, is governed completely by the single trope of metaphor. The trope of irony is closed to the myth. Irony is the trope typical of philosophy because it not only carries the meaning of one thing into another as does the metaphor, it critically juxtaposes one kind of meaning (the literal) against another that is expressed only by implication. To grasp an irony is to realize that it intends a meaning beyond what is said. An irony acts against literal-mindedness. But the myth means exactly what is said in that it is mimetic. The mythic is not and cannot as such be philosophic.

If the above is the standard view of the ancient quarrel, what further is implicit in Cassirer's approach? Cassirer with Hegel, the great philosopher

7. Plato, *Republic*, 386c.
8. Ibid., 608a.

of opposites, knows that the strongest and most antagonistic oppositions depend upon the fact that such oppositions share an unstated common factor. The common factor in the ancient quarrel is that both poetry and philosophy are mimetic. Philosophy requires *mimesis* just as much as does poetry but it requires it in a different way. Poetry's *mimesis* is of what is seen by the bodily eye—the object that can be sensed. Philosophy's *mimesis* is of what is seen only by the mind's eye—the form (*eidos*) that can be noetically grasped and upon which the reality of the sensible object depends. The mind when philosophically employed imitates the forms in its thoughts and in the way it employs language to express them. The poet and the philosopher are both imitators. Poetic wisdom can be so easily mistaken for philosophic wisdom because the image gives symbolic form to the sensible object and the sensible object is thus taken up into mind. Yet the sensible object is not fully taken up into mind because what accounts for its own ultimate reality is not explicitly present in the image. The ultimate reality of the object, for Plato, requires the power of noetic vision to imitate in thought and language the thing as it truly is.

Had Plato himself made the mimetic sense of philosophy more explicit, the necessity of preserving the validity of both sides of the quarrel might have been realized at the beginning of Western philosophy. It would have been apparent that philosophical thought requires the image as the initial means of access to the noetic, and that in the production of philosophy this dialectic of image and idea must constantly be renewed. The key to philosophical education would then have been seen to be aesthetic experience that passes beyond itself and confronts itself in the metaphysical experience of the form. This dialectical sense of *mimesis* is not what emerged from the quarrel and the agenda of Western philosophy was set in terms of the need for poetry to defend itself from philosophy and philosophy to separate itself ever further from the poetic. Cassirer asks: "Have these blames, cast on the educational value of art, ever been refuted? In the whole history of aesthetics we find the continuous echo of Plato's accusations. It became one of the most important tasks of every theory of art to refute or at least to enfeeble the Platonic arguments."[9]

Cassirer sees the attempt to meet Plato's accusations against art as beginning immediately with Aristotle. Here he also suggests an original approach. He interprets Aristotle's doctrine of *catharsis* as intended to show that art does not simply stir the emotions but is a way to calm and manage

---

9. Cassirer, *Symbol, Myth, and Culture*, 198.

them. As Aristotle says in the *Politics* that when heard by persons in ecstasy sacred songs have the effect of calming these persons "as though they had gone through a medical cure and a catharsis."[10] In Greek ethics, this state of calmness is designated by the term *euthymia*, which refers to an inner harmony of the soul, an ultimate form of compromise. Aristotle accepts the view that art depends on *mimesis*, even using it in the *Poetics* as a definition of man: "Imitation is natural to man from childhood, one of his advantages over the lower animals being this, that he is the most imitative creature in the world, and learns first by imitation."[11] Cassirer regards Aristotle's doctrine of *catharsis* as neither primarily a moral nor a psychological approach to art. He regards it as an understanding of how art is active and not passive on its audience. It is a doctrine of how the emotions are vitalized by the artwork. This vitalization depends upon the way aesthetic form can affect the emotions. Thus Aristotle does not reduce art to the emotions. His concern is how aesthetic form as distinct from the emotions can causally affect them.

Modern Aesthetics: *Liricità*

Cassirer says, "The history of aesthetics seems constantly to oscillate between two opposite poles—between an intellectual and an emotional approach to art. The former prevails in all the classical and neo-classical theories of art; the second seems now accepted by most of our modern theories."[12] The classical and neo-classical conception of art as mimetic begins to break down at the beginning of the eighteenth century. The French critic Charles Batteux, *Les beaux arts réduits à un même principe* (1747) defends the theory of imitation in general but questions whether lyrical poetry is truly imitation and asks whether it is not more correctly enthusiasm. The decisive turning point in this issue Cassirer finds in Rousseau's treatise on education, his *Nouvelle Héloïse*. On Rousseau's view the mimetic principle of art representing the world must give way to art as the manifestation of our deepest passions. On Rousseau's view the real meaning of art can only be found through this approach and the prototype of this emotional sense of art can be found in lyrical art.

---

10. Aristotle, *Politics*, 1342a.
11. Ibid., 1448b6–9.
12. Cassirer, *Symbol, Myth, and Culture*, 204.

The Aesthetic Dimension of Education

The central representative of lyricism (*liricità*) as the basis of art in modern philosophy is Benedetto Croce, *Aesthetic as Science of Expression and General Linguistic*. Cassirer also regards R. G. Collingwood's *Principles of Art* as holding the same essential position as Croce's grounding of art in the phenomenon of lyrical expression. Cassirer is often in his general idealistic approach to history and culture associated with Croce and Collingwood but in aesthetics Cassirer is strongly critical of their position.[13] Cassirer finds Croce's theory correct in that it rejects both the imitative and the hedonistic theories of art. But in equating art with expression Croce is unable to differentiate between the mere fact of expression and the mode of expression. Cassirer claims not all acts of expression are works of art. Anyone can express feelings in passionate ways but such expressions are not properly works of art. Art involves not only the expression of emotion; it also involves a constructive process in which the emotions involved are finely formed.

Cassirer's criticism of Croce presupposes the theory of expression that Cassirer develops in the third volume of the *Philosophy of Symbolic Forms*. Cassirer presents a complete phenomenology of knowledge (*Erkenntnis*) that originates in the "expressive function" (*Ausdrucksfunktion*) of consciousness. At the level of the phenomenon of expression the perceptual immediacy of the world is captured by the power of the image. Cassirer says: "For what 'is' in the object in its expressive character is not taken up and destroyed in the image; on the contrary, it is set in high relief and intensified. The image frees this expressive reality from all merely accidental determinations and concentrates it in a single focus."[14] The symbolic form that corresponds to the expressive function is myth, "the mythical world of forms shows us a way to the understanding of the phenomena of pure expression."[15] Expression does not represent a world of objects; it presents the contents of the world in a flow of images. Consciousness has no distance from this immediacy of images; its reality is the same as its images.

When the image begins to separate into itself and its object the world of the thing and the thing-symbolized arises in consciousness. This separation brings about the representational function of consciousness (*Darstellungsfunktion*). The symbolic form that corresponds to this function is language. Language for Cassirer refers to a form of consciousness that orders the

---

13. Ibid., 156–57; 206–9; 190–91.
14. Cassirer, *Philosophy of Symbolic Forms*, 3:69.
15. Ibid., 3:70.

world in terms of thing-attribute, subject-object, and symbol-symbolized. It is representational and referential thinking. Language produces what we ordinarily regard as our common sense world, which is embodied in the principles of Aristotelian class logic and descriptive-discursive forms of thought instead of imagistic renderings of experience. Croce by equating aesthetic with general linguistic as the title of his work announces cannot adequately distinguish between myth, language, and art. They all are expressive as opposed to purely cognitive or theoretical thought. Cassirer's phenomenology of theoretical thought involves his third function of consciousness, that of signification (*reine Bedeutungsfunktion*). Theoretical or scientific knowledge is built up through systems of symbols. Such purely scientific consciousness goes beyond the representational function of the words of language that refer to things. The key to purely theoretical thought is the idea of mathematical formulae and the power of formal thinking to develop levels of symbolic order.

The concept of the object at the level of the significative function of consciousness is that of $\phi(x)$ in which x stands for any series of variables and ϕ stands for the principle by which the x-series is ordered or generated. The bond between these two levels of symbols is inseparable because each has no meaning in itself. Only when both function together is there a meaningful thought pattern. The order here is not simply linear because the ϕ element can stand to another level of symbolism as a part of its (x) and in like manner the original (x) can function as a ϕ or principle of order in a sub-series.[16] This conception of the significative or scientific symbol is crucial for Cassirer's conception of art as a symbolic form.

Art arises in consciousness only when consciousness has freed itself from the empirical sense of the world that Cassirer identifies with language. The art object is not the thing and its attributes of language and the representational function of consciousness that language requires. The artist creates the art object by moving away from the purely empirical object. The artist can use language to create literature but in so doing the referential and representational power of language is transformed such that linguistic symbolism can produce a "fiction." In like manner the subject-object relationship is altered such that the artist in the art object produces subjectivity as a kind of objectivity. What is symbolized in art is generated from the process of symbolization itself in a sense analogous to the $\phi(x)$ bond of purely theoretical thinking.

16. Ibid., 3:301.

The Aesthetic Dimension of Education

The Place of Art and Myth in Culture

Cassirer through his phenomenology of the three functions of consciousness can distinguish myth from art, two forms that are often conflated in aesthetic theory. The mythical imagination remains at the level of immediacy. Myth regards all of its images as categorical truths. All primal myths present themselves as true and complete stories about the nature of the world, gods, and man. By contrast the aesthetic imagination regards its images as "hypothetical" rather than "categorical" truths. A mythical account of human nature is a complete account of man as such. A novel, poem, drama, sculpture, or painting of a human subject offers us an aspect of the human condition, a version of it that has been freely constructed. As Cassirer puts it in *Language and Myth*: "The [artistic] spirit lives in the word of language and in the mythic image without falling under the control of either. What poetry expresses is neither the mythic word-picture of gods and daemons, nor the logical truth of abstract determinations and relations."[17] Art is a form of deliberate self-knowledge: "This liberation is achieved not because the mind throws aside the sensuous forms of word and image, but in that it uses them both as organs of its own, and thereby recognizes them for what they really are: forms of its own self-revelation."[18] Art cannot occur until consciousness reaches the level of science, the level in which consciousness can deliberately construct its object (aesthetical or theoretical).

Art is a counterpart of science as a symbolic form to the extent that both art and science presuppose the power consciously to make a version of the world in symbols. Art is the realization of the subjective. Science is the realization of the objective. Science in principle eliminates all subjectivity in its constructions. Unlike art its constructions must fit what is in the world. Cassirer says that one of the principal aims of scientific thought is the elimination of all personal and anthropomorphic elements in its theories. He says: "In the words of Bacon, science strives to conceive the world '*ex analogia universi*,' not '*ex analogia hominis*.'"[19] Cassirer differentiates science, morality, and art in terms of how each produces a different form of order. He says: "Science gives us order in thoughts; morality gives us order in actions; art gives us order in the apprehension of visible, tangible,

---

17. Cassirer, *Language and Myth*, 99.
18. Ibid.
19. Cassirer, *Essay on Man*, 228.

and audible appearances"[20] Both science and art on Cassirer's view are forms of human knowledge: "art may be described as knowledge, but art is knowledge of a peculiar and specific kind."[21] Scientific truth consists in the explanation and theoretical description of things. Art consists in the intensification and sympathetic grasp of things.

As a symbolic form Cassirer insists that art has its own inner form that differentiates it from the other forms in the spectrum of cultural activity. There is no one form of cultural activity that gives us access to what the object is in itself. No one form of our experience is more "symbolic" than is another. All forms of human experience occur through the medium of the symbol whether those symbols are mythic images, words of natural language, or numbers and signs of mathematical and scientific theories.

Educational Ideals

If art may be understood as a symbolic form having a place in Cassirer's general philosophy of culture, what is the educational value of art? If as Cassirer claims all aesthetic theories are responses to this Platonic question, what is the Cassirerian answer? In Cassirer's philosophy of human culture there is a philosophy of human education that remains implicit but Cassirer never makes it truly explicit. At the end of his lecture on "The Educational Value of Art" he declares that art is "an essential and indispensable element in the system of liberal education." He says: "Art is a way to freedom, the process of the liberation of the human mind which is the real and ultimate aim of all education; it has to fulfill a task of its own, a task that cannot be replaced by any other function."[22] At the end of *An Essay on Man* he says, "Human culture taken as a whole may be described as the process of man's progressive self-liberation."[23] Implicit in Cassirer's conception of art as symbolic form in human culture, are four principal claims that can function as ideals for a conception of human education in regard to art: (1) art is an act of human freedom; (2) art is separate from morality; (3) art is a counterpart to science; and (4) art is myth remembered. I wish to emphasize that these are ideals and as ideals they are guides to understanding and action. The principles necessary to their realization are not given in

20. Ibid., 168.
21. Ibid., 169.
22. Cassirer, *Symbol, Myth, and Culture*, 215.
23. Cassirer, *Essay on Man*, 228.

Cassirer's account. Their power lies in the fact that before any value can be consciously realized, it must be idealized. The ideal provides direction and therein is its virtue.

In regard to the first, Cassirer, like Hegel, as discussed earlier, understands human freedom as self-determination. Freedom is not freedom from certain restrictions or limitations. Freedom is the power to set conditions, to act in one's own terms in relation to what is possible. The artwork is something made. It is the product of what Cassirer, as discussed in Chapter 1, calls the "basis phenomenon" of "the work" or *das Werk*. *Werk* as opposed to *Arbeit* or ordinary labor entails the production of an object. The aim of this production is self-knowledge. The human self is shaped through its ability to make its world. Cassirer says: "Know your *work* and know 'yourself' *in* your work; know what you do, so you can do what you know. Give shape to what you do . . . a work in which you recognize yourself as the sole creator and actor."[24] The artwork in its making and in its remaking by those who would comprehend it is an embodiment of the fundamental human phenomenon of *Werk*.

In regard to the second, Cassirer denies that art has a purpose outside itself. Its purpose is not morality nor is art inherently corruptive of moral sensibility. Art is a way of forming the emotions and of awakening feeling within the limits of its type of formation. Art orders our perceptions. Morality orders our actions as mentioned above. This sense of art as symbolic form is different than the claim of "art for art's sake," a view Cassirer does not accept. Art for Cassirer is rooted in common experience. It does not require special sensibilities such that art is seen as an experience open only to artists and connoisseurs. Art is expression but it is not simply expression. It is expression formed as a knowledge of the world as sensed. Morality begins from a sense of the difference between good and evil, right and wrong, just and unjust and forms an understanding of human action in terms of these. Art can pose moral problems but it does so not because of its self-identity as art but because the aesthetic and the moral both exist within culture. The moral and the aesthetic stand to each other in the same way as Cassirer says all the symbolic forms stand to each other within culture as opposites and at the same time as compliments or, as he puts it, as "harmony in contrariety."[25]

---

24. Cassirer, *Philosophy of Symbolic Forms*, 4:186.
25. Cassirer, *Essay on Man*, 228.

In regard to the third, Cassirer holds that art arises within human culture in a dialectical relation to science. He says, "In art we do not conceptualize the world, we perceptualize it."[26] Theoretical thought directs the mind toward concepts, art directs the mind toward perceptions. Art stands to science as subject to object. The practice of science teaches us to approach the world by attempting to eliminate the subjective. In this way science achieves a type of universality independent of the personality of its practitioners and of the particular culture in which scientific truths are achieved. We can speak of Chinese art, Indian art, Eskimo art, European art, etc. but we cannot do the same with science. Scientific truth does not in principle vary from culture to culture. This invariance and objectivity is the ideal of scientific inquiry. Art is the objectification of the subjective of the artist's consciousness and the consciousness of a particular culture. The self encounters its inner life in all of its manifold forms. Without art and the particularity of aesthetic form the self would lose itself in the being of the world. Art and science are necessary counterparts in the life of the self. To ignore the education of the self in its powers to feel and perceptualize is as dangerous to the full life of the self as it is to ignore the importance of its powers to theorize and conceptualize the world scientifically.

In regard to the fourth, Cassirer makes a fundamental distinction between art and myth. Myth is tied to the immediacy of the object. In mythic consciousness the world and the word are held on the same level of actuality. At the level of the myth and the mythic ritual the dancer wearing the mask of the god does not represent the god whose being is elsewhere, the dancer literally is the god. The dancer's being and the god's are immediately one. As consciousness gains distance from the world it gains in the power of self-determination. Distance from the object allows for the freedom of the self to develop its purely subjective powers. This sense of subjectivity is the basis of the artist's ability deliberately to give form to feeling and emotion, not simply too respond to expression but actively to shape it. But with the emergence of the aesthetic stance comes also a loss, the loss of the power of the origin. Art is always consciously or unconsciously an attempt at recovery of what is immediately present in the myth. The original truths of the myth are the meanings that art is always renewing in novel ways. Art is our most direct access to them. Once the immediacy of mythic expression is left behind it can only be partially recovered and without art we would forget it.

26. Cassirer, *Symbol, Myth, and Culture*, 186.

In what sense can Cassirer claim to have offered an answer to the ancient Platonic quarrel with the poets and artists? Cassirer's reconception of the philosophical problem of form from the Platonic one of the forms (*eidē*) as transcendent of the sensible to the Kantian one of form as transcendental based on the symbolic pregnance of the sensible, allows Cassirer to claim that philosophers should go to school with the poets. The quarrel of Platonic idealism with the poets is a quarrel with mythical thought. Once myth is seen as a thought-form of the original, the primordial form of the symbolic act, it becomes the starting point for all acts of consciousness and thought and it is the indispensable starting point. Transcendental idealism can acknowledge as many forms of knowledge as there are symbolic forms. Each has its own reality that is in dialectical relationship with the others. Cassirer from the perspective of his philosophy of symbolic forms has projected in modern terms the possibility of a positive connection between philosophy and poetry originally precluded in the agenda of Western philosophy as described at the end of the section on the ancient quarrel above.

Cassirer accepts both the mimetic and the emotional conceptions of art in a modified form. He accepts the mimetic view that art is a form of knowledge but modifies this knowledge claim in terms of his conception of the symbol. Art is knowledge not simply in regard to the fact that the symbol can capture what is apprehended by the senses but because the symbol has the power of the imagination to modify the object into new and novel senses of itself. Art is not reducible to emotion. Art is the active formation of emotion. The work of art shapes the world in terms of emotion and orders the object in a new way. We see the object as if for the first time and in this way a kind of knowledge is achieved. Cassirer accepts the truth that is in both the mimetic and emotional views of art and through the principles of his philosophy of culture produces the idea of art as symbolic form.

Conclusion

Cassirer's aesthetic analysis understands art as the result of three different kinds of imagination: "the power of invention, the power of personification, and the power to produce pure sensuous forms."[27] The artist invents an object. The artist does not simply imitate what is found in nature. The art object is the product of the artist's subjectivity, the artist's persona. In this sense it is a personification. What the artist produces is not something

27. Cassirer, *Essay on Man*, 164.

irrational or unnatural; it is something distinctively human, an act of self-knowledge. The artist produces pure sensuous forms. The artist uses the distinctive power of the imagination to bring before consciousness an object that is sensuous. The art object although not a direct product of the senses appears to consciousness as if it were such. The form of the art object is organic. It is a whole, the elements of which are not truly separable from their function in the whole. The organicity of the art object is responsible for its vitality. It is as if it is alive. It has a living quality. Its living quality comes not just from the organicity of its form but from the fact that the art object forms and projects human emotions. The art object is perceived, felt, and thought.

The artist not only requires the three powers of the imagination, the audience or recipient of the art object also requires them to grasp fully what the artist has produced. The recipient must participate in the artistic invention and personification and finally grasp the form. The form of the art object is what makes it a subjective universal. The form makes it more than a unique particular; its form is responsible for its universal meaning. But the form is not separable from its particular sensuous and emotional content. The form allows the artist to make and its recipient to experience a unique object that is the art object. The great artist is a master of this sense of form. This unique sense of form is what imbeds the work of the great artist in consciousness such that after Dante, Shakespeare, and Goethe, Italian, English, and German are not the same as they were before them, and after Michelangelo and Palladio our vision and sense of space is changed. The educational role of art rests on its power to cause the imagination to invent, personify, and form experience in this way. Art is a process in which the self confronts the inner world of subjectivity and forms it as an object accessible in the distinctively human world of culture. Cassirer's approach suggests that a philosophy of art cannot be self-grounded but that any philosophical comprehension of art, any aesthetic theory ultimately requires grounding in a full philosophy of human culture.

We may conclude, then, that aesthetic theory as educational theory cannot be pursued sui generis but must be connected to an understanding of human culture as a whole. Art is one of the ways in which the self determines itself by confronting the various possible forms of its existence. Moral norms can find embodiments in art but art has its own intrinsic value for the self in its process to educate itself, to acquire the inner life that is the life of the mind that characterizes the educated person. As we have seen, this process of the education of the whole person is not equivalent simply to the acquisition of knowledge. The acquisition of knowledge is not the same as the acquisition of culture. As discussed from various perspectives in the previous chapters, culture in the sense of *Bildung* is what the individual needs to develop a sense of the moral life—to bring moral philosophy together with a sense of moral education.

8

Education for the Common Good

Education can be understood in two senses. One sense is to conceive of education as the training of the mind in a specific set of subject matters and methods of investigation associated with them. The aim of education in this sense is for the individual, simply and directly, to acquire knowledge. This sense of education is not usually conceived as the pursuit of knowledge for its own sake but as the pursuit of knowledge in order to apply it to specific problems. To have knowledge of a subject matter is of great value. There is satisfaction in the acquisition of specific knowledge and in its possession for potential use.

As mentioned at the beginning of this work, a second sense of education is that expressed in the ancient Greek term *paideia*. It is a difficult term to define, as it comprehends in its meaning education not only in the sense of acquiring knowledge but in the further sense of acquiring culture and tradition. Education in the sense of *paideia* aims at producing in the individual a broad and cultivated outlook combined with the ideal of self-knowledge. Education in this sense also has a practical aim—that of the formation of the good individual.

In conclusion, regarding the views that have been put forth throughout the earlier chapters of this work, let us turn to Vico as a final guide. Vico advocates this second sense of education and connects it with the study of the whole cycle of the fields of human learning. He follows Quintilian's doctrine of the ideal orator who is "to complete the course of learning which the Greeks call *enkyklios paideia*."[1] *Enkyklios paideia* is "general education" and is the phrase from which the modern term "encyclopaedia" originates. Hellenistic and Roman writers understand this phrase as covering a range of literary and mathematical studies conceived as forming a whole. Educa-

---

1. Quintilian, *Institutio oratoria*, 1.10.1.

tion is not to be simply the mastery of some subject or set of subjects, but to be a training of the mind and spirit as a whole. Vitruvius, in describing the education needed for the production of architects, points out that such persons must be able to hold in recollection a large number of subjects. This requirement, he says, may seem quite difficult but less so when it is realized that these subjects are related to one another and have points of contact. He says: "For a general education [*encyclios enim disciplina*] is put together like one body from its members."[2] The body of human knowledge is a single corpus, a whole of its parts.

Vico pursues this concept of knowledge and human education in a unique way in his oration, "On the Heroic Mind" (*De mente heroica*), as remarked on in Chapter 6. For Vico, the heroic mind combines the pursuit of wisdom with the pursuit of eloquence. The love of learning involves a love of language because human knowledge exists in words and through words. Human education has the heroic as an ideal because the aim of such education is to bring together thought, action, and speech. To be educated is to think well, to act well, and to speak well. Heroic education requires us to grasp the interconnections of all the disciplines, not simply to specialize in one of them. Vico says: "For this task your guide will be the very nature of the human mind which rejoices in the highest degree in that which forms a unity, comes together, falls into its proper place; as witness the Latin, which seems to have derived *scientia*—that pregnant noun—from the same root that *scitus* comes from, meaning the same thing as 'beautiful.'"[3]

Vico's *New Science* contains a concept of the hero. In Vico's "ideal eternal history," each nation passes through three ages: an age of gods, in which all activities of nature and basic human institutions are associated with certain gods; an age of heroes, in which all virtues and ideals necessary for civil wisdom are embodied in the personae and deeds of heroes; and an age of humans, in which the nation declines, thought becomes abstract, losing its roots in imagination, and society loses its vital connection to custom and becomes a collection of persons held together by rights and legalism. This third age is Vico's critique of modernity. In it, the figure and the actions of the hero are no longer possible. We live, as did Vico, in the conditions of this third age, what Vico sees as the *ricorso* of Western history.

What are the characteristics of heroic mentality? The explanation of these characteristics, which Vico claims to be a wholly new subject in

---

2. Vitruvius, *De architectura*, 1.1.12.
3. Vico, "Heroic Mind," 239.

pedagogy, is the theme of his oration. In a sense it remains new, because what Vico states as the meaning of education is continually forgotten and lost in the modern workings of education, with its tendencies toward technique and specialization. In modern terms, Vico is an interdisciplinary thinker who wishes to bring together each discipline, each area of culture, and the values of each culture into a whole. Vico says, "the whole is really the flower of wisdom."[4] It is an impossible but necessary ideal—hence Vico's term, "heroic." The important point, in Vico's view, is to understand the ideal; without this understanding nothing can be done. An ideal, like a virtue, guides human action at every moment.

In advancing his concept of the heroic mind as the ideal of human education, Vico's transfers the Greek view of hero from Achilles to Socrates. Of the four cardinal virtues that Plato delineates in the *Republic* and associates with the parts of the individual psyche and the state, the first two—courage and wisdom (the others being moderation and justice)—are embodied in Achilles and Socrates, respectively.[5] The Homeric Achilles is the full figure of the spirited part of the psyche, the heroic actor. Socrates is the heroic thinker. It is not what Socrates does that affects us but what he says, the questions he asks and the "likely stories" he relates.

The heroic mind is a unique Vichian idea, but one with which Hegel and Cassirer agree and which is consistent with the spirit of the tradition of philosophical idealism. When the age of heroes has past, the heroic can remain in those actions governed by the virtue of courage, but the heroic as a way of life is not possible. What is possible is a heroism of thought, the pursuit of the contemplative life. Wisdom is the virtue that guides us to know what is beneficial for each part of the psyche and for the whole composed of the community of these parts. Wisdom is required for the common good of the psyche and society. It paves the way and culminates in the sense of proportion realized by the combination of moderation (*sophrosyne*) and justice (*dikaiosyne*). There is a courage of thought that we find in Socrates' temperament but this courage is different from that of Achilles' temperament that guides him as the crucial figure of the Trojan war. As an ideal of human education, Vico's heroic mind goes beyond a theory of learning. The ideal of the heroic mind as an aim of education points to the power of education to transform the individual into a one who connects knowledge with virtue.

4. Ibid., 77.
5. Plato, *Republic*, 442b–d.

Vico claims it is only because of the divine nature of the human mind that we can undertake the ideal of heroic education. He says that "'hero' is defined by philosophers as one who seeks ever the sublime."[6] Vico's model for the philosopher is always Socrates, who, Cicero says: "was the first to call philosophy down from the heavens and set her in the cities of men and bring her also into their homes and compel her to ask questions about life and morality and things good and evil."[7] Vico's Socrates is the Ciceronean Socrates who does not separate eloquence from knowledge, even though he is against the Sophists who misuse rhetoric. The dialectical questioning of Socrates takes thought to a level where language breaks down and insight into the true nature of the subject is produced. If "wisdom is the knowledge of things divine and human and acquaintance with the cause of each of them," as Cicero also says,[8] Socrates stands between these two realms, enabling thought to look both ways. Thought occupies this sublime position.

Vico may have in mind also Longinus, *On the Sublime*, for the source of Socrates's sublimity is surely the first principle of Longinus's doctrine that the sublime "consists in a consummate excellence and distinction of language."[9] It must also employ his idea of grandeur or the sense of synthesis, of making a whole of all that is said such that dignity is achieved. Longinus says "sublimity is the true ring of a noble mind."[10] He says, "a well-timed flash of sublimity scatters everything before it like a bolt of lightning and reveals the full power of the speaker at a single stroke."[11] To be educated is not only to acquire knowledge; it is to speak well such that mind and heart are joined. The heroic mind is a noble mind shaped by a noble spirit that pursues sublimity in its studies and speech. This is opposite Descartes' ideal in the first part of the *Discourse on Method* that as long as thought is clear and intelligible it matters not whether one speaks only Low Breton (*bas breton*) and has "never learned rhetoric."[12] For Descartes, simple clarity is enough, thought need not be a whole, nor the whole put into words.

---

6. Vico, "Heroic Mind," 230.
7. Cicero, *Tusculan Disputations*, 5.4.10–11.
8. Ibid., 4.26.57.
9. Longinus, *Sublime*, 1.3.
10. Ibid., 9.2.
11. Ibid., 1.4.
12. Descartes, *Discourse*, 114.

There are three points that are crucial for the student and for proper instruction.[13] First, the student is to swear no oath to any professor. To commit oneself to one intellectual sect or another is to give up the independence of mind necessary to true education. It is a Socratic model. Socrates belongs to no school but his own. He follows his own good genius, as Vico in his autobiography says he follows his.[14] To join a particular school of thought is to believe that all the fundamental questions are solved by its position. What is left is the comfortable activity of working with other adherents to further the school. But the fundamental questions that have been put aside are the very ones that Socratic philosophy wishes to explore.

Second, the student should not become totally involved in any single period of human knowledge. Periods of human knowledge come and go. Education should take the permanent questions as its guide. Only the best books should be read. These contain the ideas that shape human knowledge over time. This is a warning not to concentrate only on the current state of knowledge.

Third, the student should realize what each discipline imparts to the others, how all the parts of knowledge form a whole. This is a principle of interdisciplinarity. The student's aim should be to acquire a comprehensive pattern of learning, a general education from which to specialize. The individual is presented with all points of view in the university. It is the individual's task to bring these together into a whole. This view is not against specialization. It is against substituting expertise in a given field for the wisdom of the whole; it is against specialization that excludes the student developing a total perspective on human knowledge and the interconnection of its parts. This is a rhetorical conception of education. The student should aspire to the heroic mind of Cicero: to be able to speak fully, that is, eloquently, on any subject as the occasion demands. We cannot realistically believe that everyone will accomplish this ideal but it is the point at which to aim. Why aim at less? Excellence is the goal of education, not mediocrity.

This view, which derives from Vico as well as the figures treated earlier in this work, brings together the Platonic conception that education is the completion of the "inner self," the soul, and the Christian conception that education is curative of corrupt human nature. Human nature, although divine, is imperfect. Education perfects human nature and takes it toward the divine. We may easily agree with Vico's words: "metaphysics will free the

---

13. Vico, "Heroic Mind," 235.
14. Vico, *Autobiography*, 133.

intellect from the prison of the senses; logic will free the reasoning power from false opinions; ethics the will from corrupt desires. Rhetoric exists to ensure that the tongue does not betray nor fail the mind, nor the mind its theme."[15]

The heroic mind is "wisdom speaking" (*la sapienza che parla*), the Renaissance ideal that brings together philosophy and rhetoric. This bond of thought and speech is not morally neutral. The aim of education is not personal gain or glory. Nor is the aim the acquisition of purely theoretical knowledge—knowledge for knowledge's sake. The pursuit of knowledge cannot properly be divorced from the pursuit of virtue. Wisdom, as the knowledge of things divine and human, is tied to the good. We can pursue the good not simply in terms of the pursuit of the Platonic Good, as an object of contemplation, but in the Neo-Platonic sense of the "common good." Education as the perfection of the soul naturally inclines the individual toward acting for the common good, once the individual is placed in the position of responsibility that an educated person can fulfill. The ancient formula still holds true—that good states require good individuals.

Although programs of social reform and good social organization are important to a good society, in the end, good individuals make a good society. The shaping of the individual is the true goal of moral education. Education that brings together mind and heart complete the individual. Individuals who complete their own human nature make good societies. Without good individuals, there is no basis for a good society. Good persons act for the common good. The common good is promoted by good thinking and good speaking, that is, persuasion done by persons accustomed to a standard of excellence. In the end, this conception of education requires the art of rhetoric directed by a vision of the good and the divine that improves and promotes the *ethos* of the individual as a member of the human community.

---

15. Vico, "Heroic Mind," 235–36.

Bibliography

Aristotle. *The Complete Works of Aristotle: The Revised Oxford Translation*. Edited by Jonathan Barnes. 2 vols. Princeton: Princeton University Press, 1984.
Arnaud, Antoine, and Pierre Nicole. *La logique ou l'art de penser: contenant, outre les règles communes, plusieurs observations nouvelles, propres à former le jugement*. Critical edition by P. Clair and F. Girbal. Paris: Presses Universitaires de France, 1965.
Bayer, Thora Ilin. *Cassirer's Metaphysics of Symbolic Forms: A Philosophical Commentary*. New Haven: Yale University Press, 2001.
Bernheimer, Richard. "Theatrum mundi." *Art Bulletin* 28 (1956) 225–47.
Berlin, Isaiah. *The Hedgehog and the Fox: An Essay on Tolstoy's View of History*. New York: Mentor, 1957.
Cassirer, Ernst. "Der Begriff der symbolischen Form im Aufbau der Geisteswissenschaften." In *Wesen und Wirkung des Symbolbegriffs*, 171–200. Darmstadt: Wissenschaftliche Buchgesellschaft, 1956.
———. *An Essay on Man: An Introduction to a Philosophy of Human Culture*. New Haven: Yale University Press, 1944.
———. *Feiheit und Form: Studien zur deutschen Geistesgeschichte*. Berlin: Bruno Cassirer, 1916.
———. *Language and Myth*. Translated by Susanne K. Langer. New York: Harper, 1946.
———. Lecture on Herder to the Yale seminar on the "Philosophy of History," December 17, 1941. Beineke Rare Book and Manuscript Library, Cassirer Papers GEN MSS 98, Box 48, Folder 951.
———. *Leibniz' System in seinen wissenschaftlichen Grundlagen*. Darmstadt: Wissenschaftliche Buchgesellschaft, 1962.
———. *The Logic of the Cultural Sciences: Five Studies*. Translated by S. C. Lofts. New Haven: Yale University Press, 2000.
———. *The Myth of the State*. New Haven: Yale University Press, 1946.
———. *The Philosophy of the Enlightenment*. Translated by Fritz C. A. Koelln and James P. Pettegrove. Boston: Beacon, 1955.
———. *The Philosophy of Symbolic Forms*. Translated by Ralph Manheim. 3 vols. New Haven: Yale University Press, 1953–57.
———. *The Philosophy of Symbolic Forms*. Vol. 4, *The Metaphysics of Symbolic Forms*. Edited by John Michael Krois and Donald Phillip Verene. Translated by John Michael Krois. New Haven: Yale University Press, 1996.
———. *The Problem of Knowledge: Philosophy, Science, and History since Hegel*. Translated by W. H. Woglom and C. W. Hendel. New Haven: Yale University Press, 1950.

Bibliography

———. *Substance and Function*. Translated by William Curtis Swabey and Marie Collins Swabey. Chicago: Open Court, 1923.

———. *Symbol, Myth, and Culture: Essays and Lectures of Ernst Cassirer, 1935–1945*. Edited by Donald Phillip Verene. New Haven: Yale University Press, 1979.

Cicero. *De officiis*. Translated by Walter Miller. Cambridge: Harvard University Press, 2001.

———. *De oratore*. Translated by E. W. Sutton and H. Rackham. Cambridge: Harvard University Press, 2001.

———. *Topica*. Translated by H. M. Hubbell. Cambridge: Harvard University Press, 2000.

———. *Tusculan Disputations*. Translated by J. E. King. Cambridge: Harvard University Press, 2001.

Descartes, René. *The Philosophical Writings of Descartes*. Translated by John Cottingham, Robert Stoothoff, and Dugald Murdoch. 3 vols. Cambridge: Cambridge University Press, 1984.

Dewey, John. *Experience and Nature*. New York: Dover, 1958.

———. *Human Nature and Conduct*. New York: Holt, 1922.

———. *Logic, The Theory of Inquiry*. New York: Holt, 1938.

Ellul, Jacques. *The Technological Society*. Translated by John Wilkinson. New York: Knopf, 1964.

Fisch, Max Harold. "Introduction." In *The Autobiography of Giambattista Vico*, translated by Max Harold Fisch and Thomas Goddard Bergin, 1–104. Ithaca, NY: Cornell University Press, 1983.

Gadamer, Hans-Georg. *Truth and Method*. Translated by Joel Weinsheimer and Donald G. Marshall. 2nd rev. ed. New York: Crossroad, 1992.

Grassi, Ernesto. "Remarks on German Idealism, Humanism, and the Philosophical Function of Rhetoric." *Philosophy and Rhetoric* 19 (1986) 125–33.

———. *Rhetoric as Philosophy: The Humanist Tradition*. Translated by John Michael Krois and Azizeh Azodi. 2nd ed. Carbondale: Southern Illinois University Press, 2001.

Hamburg, Carl. H. "A Cassirer-Heidegger Seminar." *Philosophy and Phenomenological Research* 25 (1964) 213–22.

Hegel, G. W. F. *Aesthetics: Lectures on Fine Art*. Translated by T. M. Knox. 2 vols. Oxford: Clarendon, 1998.

———. *Briefe von und an Hegel*. Edited by Johannes Hoffmeister. 4 vols. Hamburg: Meiner, 1952–60.

———. "Das Älteste Systemprogramm des Deutschen Idealismus." In vol. 1 of *Werke*, 234–36. Frankfurt am Main: Suhrkamp, 1986.

———. *Hegel's Phenomenology of Spirit*. Translated by A. V. Miller. Oxford: Clarendon, 1977.

———. *Science of Logic*. Translated by A. V. Miller. London: Allen and Unwin, 1969.

Hume, David. *A Treatise of Human Nature*. Edited by L. A. Selby-Bigge. Oxford: Clarendon, 1960.

Juvenal. *Juvenal and Persius*. Edited and translated by Susanna Morton Braund. Cambridge: Harvard University Press, 2004.

Kant, Immanuel. *Critique of Judgment*. Translated by J. H. Bernard. New York: Hafner, 1951.

———. *Critique of Pure Reason*. Translated by Norman Kemp Smith. London: Macmillan, 1958.

Bibliography

Kroeber, A. L., and Clyde Kluckhohn. *Culture: A Critical Review of Concepts and Definitions*. New York: Vintage, 1952.
Langer, Susanne. *Philosophical Sketches*. New York: Mentor, 1964.
Longinus. *On the Sublime*. Translated by W. H. Frye. Cambridge: Harvard University Press, 1995.
Marcus Aurelius. Edited and translated by C. R. Haines. Cambridge: Harvard University Press, 2003.
Plato. *Complete Works*. Edited by John M. Cooper. Indianapolis: Hackett, 1997.
Quintilian, *Institutio oratoria*. Translated by Donald A. Russell. Cambridge: Harvard University Press, 2001.
Schilpp, Paul Arthur, ed. *The Philosophy of Ernst Cassirer*. Evanston, IL: Library of Living Philosophers, 1949.
Seneca. *Epistles*. Translated by Richard M. Gunnaere. 3 vols. Cambridge: Harvard University Press, 2001.
———. *Moral Essays*. Translated by J. W. Basore. 3 vols. Cambridge: Harvard University Press, 2001.
Shaftesbury, Anthony Ashley Cooper, Third Earl of. *Characteristicks of Men, Manners, Opinions, Times*. Vol. 1. Indianapolis: Liberty Fund, 2001.
Smith, John H. *The Spirit and Its Letter: Traces of Rhetoric in Hegel's Philosophy of "Bildung"*. Ithaca, NY: Cornell University Press, 1988.
Stirling, James Hutchinson. *The Secret of Hegel*. Rev. ed. New York: Putnam, 1887.
Verene, Donald Phillip. *Hegel's Absolute: An Introduction to Reading the "Phenomenology of Spirit"*. Albany: State University of New York Press, 2007.
———. *Hegel's Recollection: A Study of Images in the "Phenomenology of Spirit"*. Albany: State University of New York Press, 1985.
———. "Vico's Influence on Cassirer." *New Vico Studies* 3 (1985) 105–11.
Vico, Giambattista. *The Art of Rhetoric (Institutiones oratoriae, 1711–1741)*. Translated and edited by Giorgio A. Pinton and Arthur W. Shippee. Amsterdam: Rodopi, 1996.
———. *The Autobiography of Giambattista Vico*. Translated by Max Harold Fisch and Thomas Goddard Bergin. Ithaca, NY: Cornell University Press, 1975.
———. "On the Heroic Mind." Translated by Elizabeth Sewell and Anthony C. Sirignano. In *Vico and Contemporary Thought*, edited by Giorgio Tagliacozzo, Michael Mooney, and Donald Phillip Verene, 228–45. Atlantic Highlands, NJ: Humanities, 1979.
———. *On Humanistic Education (Six Inaugural Orations, 1699–1707)*. Translated by Giorgio A. Pinton and Arthur W. Shippee. Ithaca, NY: Cornell University Press, 1993.
———. *On the Most Ancient Wisdom of the Italians*. Translated by L. M. Palmer. Ithaca, NY: Cornell University Press, 1988.
———. *The New Science of Giambattista Vico*. Translated by Thomas Goddard Bergin and Max Harold Fisch. Ithaca, NY: Cornell University Press, 1984.
———. *On the Study Methods of Our Time*. Translated by Elio Gianturco. Ithaca, NY: Cornell University Press, 1990.
———. *Universal Law*. Translated by John D. Schaeffer. 2 vols. Lewiston, NY: E. Mellen, 2011.
Vischer, Friedrich Theodor. "Das Symbol." In *Philosophische Aufsätze: Eduard Zeller, zu seinem fünfzigjährigen Doctor-Jubiläum gewidmet*. Leipzig: Fues's Verlag, 1887.
Vitruvius. *De architectura*. Translated by Frank Granger. 2 vols. Cambridge: Harvard University Press, 2004.

Bibliography

White, James Boyd. *Heracles' Bow: Essays on the Rhetoric and Poetics of the Law*. Madison: University of Wisconsin Press, 1985.

Whitehead, A. N. *The Function of Reason*. Boston: Beacon, 1962.

———. *Process and Reality: An Essay in Cosmology*. New York: Harper, 1957.

Yates, Frances A. *The Art of Memory*. Chicago: University of Chicago Press, 1966.

Index

Achilles, 28, 34, 112, 126
Aeneas, 80
Alcibiades, 105
Alembert, Jean Le Rond d', 70
Aquadies, Felice, 87
Aretino, Pietro, 33
Aristotle, 5
    on art, 113–14
    on human nature, 46–48
    on metaphor, 82–83
    on rhetoric, 67, 98–105
    on the senses, 90–95
    on the syllogism, 69
Arnauld, Antoine, 69

Bacon, Francis, 117
Batteux, Charles, 114
Bayle, Pierre, 70
Bergson, Henri, 3, 11
Berlin, Isaiah, xv, 30
Borgia, Cesare, 33
Bowne, Borden Parker, 51
Buffier, Claude, 92–93
Burckhardt, Jakob, 26, 30, 33

Caesar, Gaius Julius, Roman emperor, 23–24, 87
Camillo, Guilio, 97–98, 101
Cassirer, Ernst, xii-xiii, xv-xvi, 126
    art as symbolic form, 109–23
    criticism of Croce, 114–16
    definition of symbolic form, 20–22
    and Dewey, xiii, 36–49, 64
    philosophy of culture, 1–18
    philosophy of history, 19–35
    relation to pluralism, 50–65
    and Vico, xii-xiii, 26–32
Castor and Pollux, 96
Cicero, 87, 91
    on rhetoric, 96–99, 103–6, 128
    on Socrates, 64, 127
Cohen, Hermann, 32, 51
Collingwood, R. G., 51, 109, 115
Constantine I the Great, Roman emperor, 26
Critias, 105
Crito, 103
Croce, Benedetto, 51, 109, 115–16

Dante, 80, 122
Descartes, René, 11–12, 98
    and Vico, 30–32, 85, 89, 95, 127
    on common sense, 92–93
Dewey, John, xiii, 50, 62, 64
    concept of habit, 38–46
    concept of human nature, 36–38
    philosophy of education, 46–49
Diderot, Denis, 70
Dilthey, Wilhelm, 25, 51

Ellul, Jacques, 106

Fichte, Johann Gottlieb, 12, 61
Ficino, Marsilio, 33
Freud, Sigmund, 39

Gadamer, Hans-Georg, 92
Gianturco, Elio, 87

Index

Goethe, Johann Wolfgang von, 4, 31, 61, 71, 122
  source for "basis phenomena," 3, 8–10
  view of Plato and Aristotle, 5
Gorgias, 103, 105
Grassi, Ernesto, 81–82

Hamann, Johann Georg, 30
Hegel, G. W. F., 18, 52, 85, 112, 119, 126
  and concept of *Bildung*, 83
  doctrine of idealism, xi-xiii, 1–4, 7–8, 44, 58–59
  phenomenology, xiv-xvi, 2, 61, 66–84
  True is the whole, xiii, 54, 58
Heidegger, Martin, 3, 52
Heraclitus, 57
Hercules, 76
Herder, Johann Gottfried von, 3, 27, 30–32
Hertz, Heinrich, 3, 21
Hippias, 103
Hippocrates, xiv
Holborn, Hajo, 51
Homer, 76, 80, 110–12
Horace, 92
Howison, George Holmes, 51
Humboldt, Wilhelm von, 3, 61
Hume, David, 38, 94
Husserl, Edmund, 11–12, 56

James, William, 50, 62, 64–65
Johnson, Samuel, 15
Jove, 28, 101–2
Juno, 28
Juvenal, 91

Kant, Immanuel, xv, 10, 12, 15, 18, 61, 70–71, 76
  doctrine of idealism, xi-xii, 1–8, 23
  doctrine of thing-in-itself, 72–74
  doctrine of triadic form, 75
  and philosophy of culture, 54–55, 58–59
  theory of the sublime, 77–78
  view of rhetoric, 67, 69–70
Klages, Ludwig, 3

Langer, Susanne K., 20
Leibniz, Gottfried Wilhelm von, 15, 31–32, 61
Leonardo da Vinci, 33
Longinus, 68, 77, 79–80, 127
Lotze, Rudolf Hermann, 51–52
Luther, Martin, 76

Machiavelli, Niccolò, 33
Marcus Aurelius, 92, 94
Marx, Karl, 39
Meier, Georg Friedrich, 70
Michelangelo, 33, 122
Montaigne, Michel, 15

Natorp, Paul, 32, 51
Nicole, Pierre, 69
Nietzsche, Friedrich, 39

Odysseus, xiv-xv, 28

Palladio, Andrea, 122
Pericles, 103
Plato, 12, 66, 68, 89, 107, 126
  concept of philosophy, xiii-xv, 5, 27
  definition of "hero," 87
  quarrel with poets, xii, 27, 110–14
  and rhetoric, 103–4
Pope, Alexander, 15
Prodicus, 103
Protagoras, 103

Quintilian, 96, 103, 105–6, 124

Ranke, Leopold von, 24
Reid, Thomas, 93, 95
Rickert, Heinrich, 25, 51
Robinson Crusoe, 22, 56
Rousseau, Jean-Jacques, 31, 71, 114

Scheler, Max, 3, 52
Schelling, Friedrich Wilhelm Joseph von, xii, 61, 69
Schiller, Johann Christoph Friedrich von, 25, 71, 78
Schilpp, Paul, 110
Schweitzer, Albert, 5, 7, 18, 64

Index

Seneca, 91–92
Shaftesbury, Anthony Ashley Cooper, Third Earl of, 92–96
Shakespeare, William, 76, 122
Simmel, Georg, 3, 52
Simonides of Ceos, 96
Smith, John H., 68, 77, 83
Socrates, 106, 111, 126–28
    concept of philosophy, 10, 12–13, 14, 65, 102–5
    and rhetoric, 104–5
    and self-knowledge, 14, 16–17, 25, 36, 83
Stirling, James Hutchinson, 67, 83
Stoics, 91–94

Taine, Hippolyte, 26
Thucydides, 26–27

Uexküll, Jakob von, 39–40

Varro, Marcus Terentius, 89
Vecchio, Fabrizio del, 88

Verde, Francesco, 87
Verene, Donald Phillip, 68, 74, 82
Vergil, 80
Vico, Giambattista, xi, 31–32, 61
    Cassirer's view of, xii-xiii, 3, 13–14, 20, 34–35, 27–29, 34
    "new critical art," 29–30
    view of education, 85–108, 124–29
Vischer, Friedrich Theodor, 3, 21
Vitruvius Pollio, Marcus, 125
Voltaire (François Marie Arouet), 15, 30
Voss, Johann Heinrich, 76

Wahl, Jean, 51
Whitehead, A. N., xiv-xv, 64
Wieland, Christoph Martin, 71
Windelband, Wilhelm, 25, 51
Wölfflin, Heinrich, 33

Xenophon, 12

Yates, Frances, 72

www.ingramcontent.com/pod-product-compliance
Lightning Source LLC
Chambersburg PA
CBHW031500160426
43195CB00010BB/1038